About North
Wales

Published by Graffeg
First published 2007
Copyright © Graffeg 2007
ISBN 978 1 905582 04 4

Graffeg, Radnor Court, 256 Cowbridge
Road East, Cardiff CF5 1GZ Wales UK.
Tel: +44(0)29 2037 7312
sales@graffeg.com www.graffeg.com
Graffeg are hereby identified as the
authors of this work in accordance
with section 77 of the Copyrights,
Designs and Patents Act 1988.

Distributed by the Welsh Books
Council www.cllc.org.uk
castellbrychan@cllc.org.uk

A CIP Catalogue record for this book
is available from the British Library.

Designed and produced by
Peter Gill & Associates
sales@petergill.com
www.petergill.com

Map base information reproduced
by permission of Ordnance Survey
on behalf of HMSO
© Crown Copyright.
All rights reserved. Ordnance Survey
Licence number 100020518

About North Wales
Written by David Williams,
foreword by Siân Lloyd

The publishers are also grateful to
the Welsh Books Council for their
financial support and marketing
advice. www.gwales.com

Every effort has been made to
ensure that the information in this
book is current and it is given in good
faith at the time of publication. Please
be aware that circumstances can
change and be sure to check details
before making travel plans.

Front cover image: Conwy Castle and
Thomas Telford's bridge.

About North
Wales

Foreword

"Whether you live here or are visiting for the first time, I hope that this book will inspire you to explore Wales's many cultural and historical treasures, leading you to new and exciting experiences. It is intended to be a source book of ideas for things to do."

Wales is a remarkable part of the world where, over many centuries, people have created a rich and fascinating heritage. From battle-worn castles to settled towns and villages, from mines and quarries to elegant historic houses, there are tremendous places to visit.

Museums draw upon wonderful original material to tell our story. Many towns have local-history museums. The National Museum Wales, an impressive group of museums and galleries, illuminates our collective past through informative and innovative displays.

Our enthusiasm for culture, especially music and literature, is famous. Wales produces stars of concert hall, opera, stage, screen and rock arena – along with gifted writers and poets. There is strength in depth, from keen amateur activity in local halls and eisteddfodau to the thriving professional sphere. Major festivals, and smaller events, accommodate every cultural and artistic activity: music, literature, theatre, dance, the visual arts and others.

Wales asserts its cultural individuality in an increasingly interconnected and globalised world. The long history of the Welsh people has evolved into a forward-looking modern identity, based on respect for the past. As someone who works in both England and Wales, and travels widely, I enjoy sharing this distinctive sense of identity with people I meet.

I am fluently bilingual in Welsh and English and thank my parents for sending me to a Welsh school. The opportunities I received there – especially in public speaking, drama and music – set me on course to become a broadcaster.

The Welsh language, spoken by around half a million people, supports a wonderful literature and a thriving culture. English and Welsh enjoy official status together and many other languages are heard too, especially in the multicultural cities of Cardiff, Swansea and Newport.

Whether you live here or are visiting for the first time, I hope that this book will inspire you to explore Wales's many cultural and historic treasures. It is intended to be a source book of ideas for things to do. So, please enjoy the evocative photographs and learn interesting things but, above all, be sure to get out and about to experience the wonders of Wales for yourself.

Siân Lloyd

Left: **Caernarfon Castle.** Intended to be a royal residence and seat of government for north Wales, the castle's status was emphasized when Edward I made sure that his son, the first English Prince of Wales, was born here in 1284.

5

Introduction

This book celebrates the historical and cultural attractions that make north Wales such a special place. We hope that it will lead you to enjoyable discoveries and a deeper appreciation of this ancient and profoundly fascinating region and its people.

Located on the western side of the UK, Wales is bounded by the sea on three sides and shares a border with England to the east. Almost a quarter of its area enjoys special environmental designation.

Our three national parks – Snowdonia, the Brecon Beacons and the Pembrokeshire Coast – contain landscapes and habitats of international importance. Other regions throughout Wales are designated Areas of Outstanding Natural Beauty and there are more than 1,000 Sites of Special Scientific Interest.

But it is the way in which people have left their mark – on the landscape, in towns and cities, and on the world – that gives Wales its unique character. It is a place where a sense of history, and the achievements of the past, are valued by an advanced modern nation.

Wales is part of the United Kingdom and therefore is not fully a nation state. But its people certainly see themselves as a distinct nation. The Welsh language reinforces this identity, yet many people who do not speak it are also quick to assert their Welshness. The devolution of significant powers from Parliament in London to the National Assembly for Wales in Cardiff has given us one of the world's newest democratic institutions and greater autonomy.

Evidence of how people lived and worked over the centuries is preserved at our many ancient monuments, castles, historic houses and industrial locations. Wales has two UNESCO World Heritage Sites: the great medieval castles and town walls of north-west Wales and the industrial landscape of Blaenavon in the south-east.

Many places are in the care of either the National Trust or CADW, the Welsh Assembly Government's historic environment division. Museums and galleries, including the National Museum Wales, tell of our remarkable past.

The Welsh are seen as musically and lyrically gifted people. Ability in the areas is celebrated at local events and major festivals. The vigorous cultural life reflects the varied origins of the people (especially in the cities) and their typically open-minded gregariousness.

This book celebrates some of the historical and cultural attractions that make north Wales such a special place. We hope that it will lead you to enjoyable discoveries and a deeper appreciation of this ancient and profoundly fascinating region and its people.

David Williams

Left: **National Eisteddfod.**
Held at the beginning of August, the National Eisteddfod moves to a different part of Wales each year.

About this book

The aim of this book is to give you a taste of some of the main cultural and historical attractions of north Wales. It is one of a series of four regional pocket guides that cover, between them, the whole of Wales.

You will find information on many locations to visit and events to enjoy: castles, historic houses, industrial-heritage sites, museums, galleries, large festivals and local gatherings.

Each entry provides guidance on how to get there. Maps show the towns and villages mentioned, and the main roads. Contact information and website addresses will enable you to find current event programmes, opening times and any admission charges, and to plan your visit in detail.

We list the best-known attractions but, of course, Wales has such a rich heritage that there are many more places to explore. The main tourism websites – and those of organisations including CADW and the National Trust – are included here.

We also provide details of Tourism Information Centres, places to stay and eat, advice on north Wales's public transport system and an introduction to the Welsh language. The book concludes with an index of places, attractions, festivals and events.

We hope you enjoy browsing in search of interesting places to visit and things to do.

North Wales
From Wales's highest peak,
Snowdon, to the dramatic coasts
of Anglesey and Llŷn, and scenic
borderlands.

Above left: **Chirk Castle.** Chirk
Castle is a 700-year old Marcher
fortress, which commands fine
views over the surrounding
countryside. It was built in the
early-14th century by Roger
Mortimer, First Earl of the March
under Edward I.
Above right: **Menai Strait.** Thomas
Telford's suspension bridge,
completed in 1826, was a huge
improvement over the ferries that
previously served the coach route
from London to Holyhead – then, as
it is today, the ferry port for Dublin.

Contents

Map 10

Anglesey 12

**Llandudno, Colwyn Bay,
Rhyl and Prestatyn** 30

North Wales Borderlands 44

**Snowdonia Mountains and
Coast** 68

Where to eat and stay 86

Information and websites 87

How to get there 88

What to see and do
throughout Wales 90

The Welsh language 114

Graffeg books 116

About the authors 117

Index 118

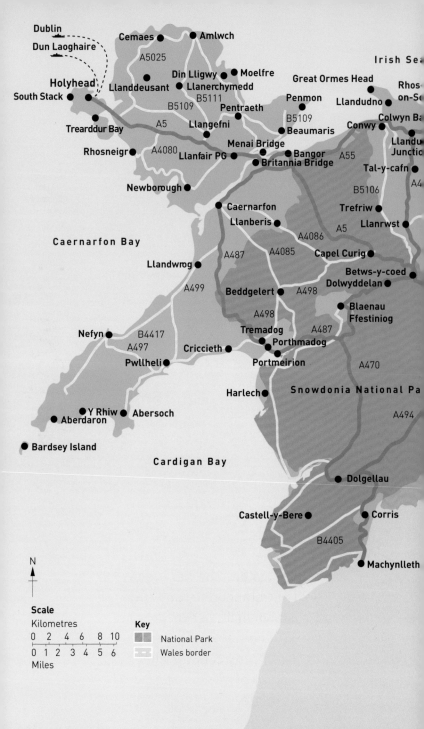

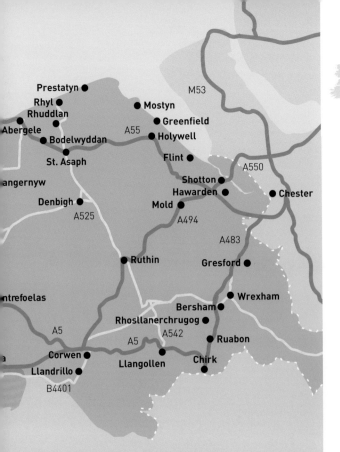

Welcome to North Wales, an enchanting area of striking contrasts. The Snowdonia National Park has the highest mountains in England and Wales. The Llŷn peninsula, the Cambrian Coast and the Isle of Anglesey are places of fascinating history and heritage. The coastal resorts of Llandudno, Colwyn Bay, Rhyl and Prestatyn include everything that is exciting about the traditional seaside. The Borderlands have pretty country villages and an impressive array of castles and historic houses to explore.

Anglesey

Beaumaris Castle, Plas Newydd, Bryn Celli Ddu,
Parys Mountain and delightful Moelfre. Cultural
highlights include Oriel Ynys Môn, Beaumaris
Festival, Ucheldre Centre and the Museum of
Childhood.

Amlwch

Amlwch Port. This intriguing harbour, a narrow, north-facing cove protected by breakwaters, was built in the late 18th century for the purpose of exporting copper from Parys Mountain. A thriving ship-building industry developed alongside this trade, reaching its peak in the late 19th century with the construction of a series of graceful schooners. The museum overlooking the harbour tells the story.

• From Amlwch, in north-eastern Anglesey, signs guide you to this remarkable place redolent of the past.
www.amlwchweb.com
(photo page 25)

Parys Mountain. During the Bronze Age copper was extracted and put to use in this north-eastern corner of Anglesey, and the Romans also mined it here. But it was the Industrial Revolution that developed new prospects and brought the demand that made Parys Mountain the largest copper mine in Europe. A trail around the vast open cast scar gives amazing vistas of deeply coloured red, purple and yellow ores. Be sure to stay on the path, away from the deep and dangerous mine excavations.

Above: **Beaumaris Castle.** The well-preserved structure of Beaumaris Castle makes an impressive sight on the shore of the Menai Strait, with the mountains of Snowdonia beyond.

• Inland from Amlwch, between the A5025 and the B5111.
Phone: 01407 832255
www.angleseyheritage.org

Moelfre – Royal Charter wreck.
A remarkable statue of Coxswain Richard Evans MBE, recipient of two RNLI gold medals for bravery, looks out over the bay from the Seawatch Centre, Moelfre. This coastline has seen many shipwrecks, including that of the sailing vessel Royal Charter. She was driven onto the rocks by a mighty storm in October 1859 within forty miles of her destination, Liverpool, at the end of a voyage from Australia. Out of 490 passengers and crew, only 40 survived. Charles Dickens visited the scene of the tragedy, which he described in 'The Uncommercial Traveller'.
• An excellent footpath, which is surfaced for wheelchairs, leads from the village past the Seawatch Centre and the lifeboat station (often open in summer) to the site of the wreck.
Phone: 01248 410277

Beaumaris

The name of this attractive coastal town derives from the Norman "beau mareys", meaning beautiful marsh. From the pier and beach, which offer spectacular views of **Snowdonia**, to the castle and the character-filled streets with their wonderful mix of medieval, Georgian, Victorian and Edwardian architecture, this is an enchanting place to explore on foot.
• Some six miles from the A55 expressway as it crosses into Anglesey along the Britannia Bridge: follow the scenic and winding A545.
www.angleseyheritage.org

Beaumaris Castle. This was the last castle built for Edward I during his campaign to subjugate the people of Gwynedd. Along with his fortresses at Caernarfon, Conwy and Harlech, it enjoys UNESCO **World Heritage Site** status. Construction began in 1295, but the money ran out and the work was never finished. It is nevertheless an outstanding example of "walls within walls" construction, generally agreed to be the most perfectly realised castle in the UK. An attacker would have to breach four lines of fortification and fourteen separate defensive obstacles, beginning with a moat, while arrows rained down from ingeniously positioned slits.
• At the end of the main street in Beaumaris. There is parking nearby on The Green, the open area of grass between the town and the Menai Strait.
Phone: 01248 810361
www.cadw.wales.gov.uk

Right: Moelfre. Sculpture of seafaring hero Coxswain Richard Evans MBE.

Beaumaris Gaol and Courthouse.
These atmospheric buildings give
an insight into the harsh justice of
times gone by. The courthouse,
built in 1614, bears an
entertaining mural showing two
farmers in dispute over the
ownership of a cow: one pulls at
its horns, the other at its tail,
while a lawyer milks away below.
The Victorian gaol, with its
gallows high on the walls, has the
only working human treadmill in
the UK.
• The historic buildings and
attractions of Beaumaris are
clearly signed and are within
walking distance of the castle.
Phone: 01248 810921 (Gaol)
Phone: 01248 811691 (Court)
www.angleseyheritage.org

**Museum of Childhood Memories,
Beaumaris.** In nine variously
themed rooms at No.1 Castle
Street – one of the impressive
Georgian houses that
characterise Beaumaris – you
will find a treasure trove of
memorabilia, toys and household
items relating to the happier
aspects of family life over the
past 150 years. The displays will
enthrall children, while bringing
back many memories for the
older generation.
• At the same end of Castle
Street as the castle, close to the
parking space on The Green.
Phone: 01248 712498
www.aboutbritain.com

Menai Suspension Bridge.
The graceful span of Thomas
Telford's suspension bridge, the
first of its type in the world on
such a scale, has been a familiar
and attractive presence amid the
scenic splendour of the Menai
Strait since 1826. On the 30th of
January of that year, the crowds
cheered as the Royal London and
Holyhead Mail Coach crossed
over to Anglesey with its
important cargo of mail bags
bound for Dublin. It is possible to
walk across the bridge – its
construction is fascinating and
the views are tremendous, while
the tide flows at a remarkable
rate through the arches.
• Narrow lanes lead down from
the Anglesey end of the bridge
to the small beach and
quayside beneath.
www.angleseyheritage.org

Britannia Bridge.
Robert Stephenson, son of
the famous railway engineer
George Stephenson, adopted an
unusual design for his rail bridge,
which was completed in 1850.
To achieve the stiffness necessary
to maintain the straightness of
the rails under the weight of a
train, while avoiding the use of an
arch and the attendant loss of
headroom for the masts of sailing
ships passing below, he built a

Left: Menai Strait. Set against the
backdrop of northern Snowdonia,
Thomas Telford's suspension bridge
across the Menai Strait occupies its
place in the landscape with
great dignity.

rectangular iron tube, similar in essence to a ship's hull. This served well until 1970, when it was accidentally set on fire. The present structure, supported by massive arches, has both rail and road decks.

• The bridges make a fine sight, set in the panorama of the Menai Strait and Snowdonia, from the top of the Marquess of Anglesey's column at Llanfair PG.
www.angleseyheritage.org

Plas Newydd. This elegant 18th century house, designed by James Wyatt and now in the care of the National Trust, is the ancestral home of the Marquess of Anglesey. It contains a magnificent 18m wide mural by **Rex Whistler** and other fine examples of his work. A military museum tells the story of the first Marquess who, having lost a leg while commanding the cavalry at the battle of Waterloo, was fitted with the first artificial leg to have sprung joints – and yes, this innovative device is on display.

• A couple of miles south-west of J8 on the A55 (for Llanfair PG), along the A4080.
Phone: 01248 714795
www.nationaltrust.org.uk

Open-air theatre at Plas Newydd. The elegance of the impressive house is just one of the attractions of Plas Newydd. The surrounding woodland and fine gardens are a pleasure to behold in any season. Summer offers the additional delights of

open-air performances of music and drama, including productions of Shakespeare.

Bryn Celli Ddu and Barclodiad y Gawres. Anglesey, with its gentle landscape, fertile soil, mild maritime climate and convenient location at the centre of Irish Sea trade routes, has been populated since prehistoric times.
The island has many important Neolithic monuments, including standing stones and burial chambers. **Barclodiad y Gawres** is a passage grave containing stones inscribed with the spiral and zigzag designs also found elsewhere in Wales and in Ireland. **Bryn Celli Ddu** is a burial chamber overlying a "henge" used for religious ceremonies.

• Barclodiad y Gawres is south of Rhosneigr, on the A4080; Bryn Celli Ddu is off a minor road between the A4080, near Plas Newydd, and the village of Llanddaniel Fab.
www.cadw.wales.gov.uk

Oriel Ynys Môn. Anglesey's main heritage centre and art gallery is conveniently located just outside Llangefni. A permanent exhibition introduces the island's rich culture and history.
An imaginative programme of

Above: **Plas Newydd.**
The attractions of Plas Newydd include the fine interiors, the woodland walk that takes you around the gardens, and the exciting programme of activities for all the family.

temporary exhibitions and events encompassing art, craft, sculpture, music and social history provides plenty of reasons to visit throughout the year. There is a café and a shop that sells local-interest books and the work of local artists, craft workers and jewellers.

• Just north of Llangefni, on the B5111 towards Llanerchymedd. Phone: 01248 724444
www.angleseyheritage.org

Llys Rhosyr, Newborough.

The independent Kingdom of Gwynedd, which emerged after the departure of the Romans and lasted until the death of Prince Llywelyn at the hands of Edward I's troops in 1282, had its power base in Anglesey. Its rulers divided their time between their courts at Aberffraw and Llys Rhosyr and their castles in Snowdonia. These foundations convey a potent sense of the loss that must have been felt as power was seized by Edward I, whose mighty castle at Caernarfon is in sight across the Menai Strait.

• Just outside the village of Newborough in southern Anglesey, along the minor road leading to Llanddwyn, near the church.
www.angleseyheritage.org

Llanfairpwllgwyngyllgogerychw-yrndrobwllllantysiliogogogoch.

Following the arrival of the railway during the 1850s, the enterprising villagers of Llanfair Pwllgwyngyll (as it was

then known) sought ways of attracting trains and early tourists. In what would today be described as a stroke of marketing genius, a cobbler from Menai Bridge invented the longest name of any village anywhere, bringing the worldwide fame that continues to this day. The name, proudly displayed on the station and village shops (and on a gift shop in Cardiff, opposite the castle), means 'Saint Mary's Church in the hollow of the white hazel near a rapid whirlpool and the church of Saint Tysilio of the red cave'.

• Leave the A55 expressway just after it crosses the Britannia Bridge onto Anglesey and follow the A5 to the village.

Holyhead

Roman fort at Holyhead.
Here, late in their history and at the far western limit of their conquests, the Romans, under increasing pressure to recall troops to defend the heart of their declining empire, built a small fort and naval base to guard against raiders from across

Above left: **Swtan restored cottage.** Swtan has the whitewashed walls typical of many cottages and farm buildings all over Anglesey (page 24). Above right: **Llys Rhosyr, Newborough.** To appreciate the significance of this atmospheric place, see the audio-visual presentation at the Pritchard Jones Institute in Newborough.

the Irish Sea. It is said that Maelgwyn, the 6th century king of Gwynedd, gave the land within the walls of the fort to St Cybi as the site for a monastery, of which the present St Cybi's church is the successor.

• In the town centre, seek out the outstanding stained glass windows by William Morris and the pre-Raphaelites.
www.holyhead.com

Ucheldre Centre, Holyhead.
Quality is the watchword at this powerhouse for the performing, literary and visual arts. Music and drama are staged in the beautiful and acoustically excellent chapel of the former Bon Sauveur convent. The adjoining exhibition gallery has an ever-changing programme of painting, sculpture and crafts, often supported by talks and classes. The licensed Ucheldre Kitchen prepares traditional recipes and the centre's shop has a good selection of books, music and gifts.

• Just outside the town centre, at Millbank, signed from the minor road past the park towards South Stack.
Phone: 01407 763361
www.ucheldre.org

Holyhead Maritime Museum.
The seafaring traditions of the port of Holyhead are celebrated at this excellent maritime museum, run by knowledgeable

volunteers and housed in the oldest lifeboat station in Wales, which dates from 1847. Displays of models, paintings, photographs and artefacts trace the town's history from Roman times to its present position as the UK's main ferry port for passenger and cargo services to Ireland.
• On Newry Beach, overlooking the large Outer Harbour, with views towards the breakwater and the ferries.
Phone: 01407 769745
www.angleseyheritage.org

Llynnon Mill. Anglesey's rich arable farmland has for many centuries produced an abundance of produce, both for local use and for sale further afield. Farmers brought wheat, barley, oats and other grains to one of the island's many windmills or watermills to be made into flour or animal feed. Llynnon is the only working windmill in Wales. The miller makes stoneground flour from organic wheat. He will be happy to explain the process and sell you a bag.
• Near Llanddeusant, signed from the A5025 and minor roads around Llanfaethlu.
Phone: 01407 730797
www.goanglesey.com

Above: **Llynnon Mill. The spinning sails of Llynnon Mill drive heavy millstones to grind flour in the traditional way, as windmills once did all over Wales.**

Swtan restored cottage. In its idyllic location at Church Bay on the west coast of Anglesey, the last traditional thatched cottage on Anglesey has been restored, and opens to the public each summer. With its cosy crogloft, where children would sleep, and large open hearth, it is typical of a style once common throughout rural Wales. Household and farm implements, and the well-tended vegetable garden give an insight into the labour intensive life of its former occupants.
• Between Llanfaethlu and Llanrhuddlad, north-east of Holyhead on the A5025: follow narrow lanes to Church Bay. www.angleseyheritage.org

Iron Age settlements – Din Lligwy and Tŷ Mawr. The circular remains of ten stone huts at Tŷ Mawr, near Holyhead, once had conical roofs supported by wooden posts and thatched with straw or reeds. The site was occupied intermittently over a very long period, from Mesolithic times until the 6th century. The much grander compound of houses and working buildings at Din Lligwy, on the eastern side of Anglesey, evolved during the Roman occupation as the local Celtic chieftain adapted to the new ways.
• Tŷ Mawr is off the minor road from Holyhead to South Stack; Din Lligwy is signed from the A5025 and minor roads near Moelfre and Llanallgo.

Penmon

A remarkable cluster of buildings and monuments surrounds the holy well of St Seiriol, who lived at Penmon during the 6th century. The church dates from the 12th century. It houses two early Celtic crosses and has impressive Romanesque decoration. The associated **Augustinian priory buildings** were added a century later, and the nearby fishpond and dovecote are evidence of the self-sufficient lifestyle of the monks.

• A pleasant drive beyond Beaumaris, along the B5109. www.angleseyheritage.org

South Stack

South Stack and Ellin's Tower. The spectacularly located lighthouse at South Stack was built in 1809 for the benefit of shipping navigating the busy Irish Sea. Buy a ticket at the South Stack Café for access to the island and a guided tour of the historic structure. The strenuous walk down, and then back up, some four hundred steps, giving magnificent close up views of seabird nesting sites, is

Above left: **South Stack.** An incomparable place for exhilarating clifftop walks. Above right: **Amlwch Port.** Built in the late 18th century.

most worthwhile. **Ellin's Tower** was built in 1868 as a summer house for the Stanley family, and named after their daughter. It is now an interpretive centre run by the Royal Society for the Protection of Birds.

• South Stack is a short drive, or a bracing walk around the mountain, from Holyhead. Ellin's Tower is off the approach road, near the café.
www.angleseyheritage.org

Festivals and events

Amlwch Viking Festival.

Every two years, around the **end of July**, Amlwch commemorates the presence of the Vikings on Anglesey. Be ready to encounter authentically dressed warriors and villagers as they re-create the rivalry on the island after Viking raids, and re-enact the battle to expel the invaders. Walk around a replica 10th century encampment, experience a Viking wedding and see craftsmen at work. Join the throngs of people at Amlwch Port to witness the ceremonial boat burning and fireworks display.

• Park away from the narrow quaysides of Amlwch Port. There are good vantage points on footpaths above the harbour.
www.amlwchvikingfestival.co.uk

Anglesey County Show.

The Anglesey County Show is held annually in **August.** It is a large event organised for the buying and selling of animals, farm vehicles, agricultural services and equipment. But earning a living from the land has been central to the identity and character of many of the island's inhabitants for centuries. The main ring and exhibition stands showcase both traditional skills and modern methods, and the show is a great place to experience the camaraderie typical of the farming community.

• Held at the County Showground near Mona, well signed from the A55.
Phone: 01407 720072
www.angleseyshow.org.uk

Anglesey Oyster and Welsh Food Fair.

Early October sees the food cognoscenti heading towards Trearddur Bay for the Anglesey Oyster and Welsh Produce Festival. There they will find a wide selection of Welsh food producers, along with a full programme of demonstrations and competitions. **Halen Môn** (Anglesey Sea Salt), **Gorau Glas** (blue cheese) and the varied delights of the **Deri Fawr smokery** are but a few examples of the wealth of fine produce grown or produced locally.

• The village and attractive beaches of Trearddur Bay are a couple of miles to the south of Holyhead, on the B4545.
www.angleseyoysterfestival.com

Left: **Celtic cross**. This fine Celtic Cross commemorates Anglesey's 18th century intellectuals, the Morris brothers.

Beaumaris Festival.
The Beaumaris Festival was founded in 1986 and has grown into a popular and prestigious event attracting international performers of the highest calibre. Held over the **May** Bank Holiday weekend, and a few days either side, it provides a feast of classical music, jazz, talks, theatre, poetry and art.
The festival also features recitals by young performers, giving audiences a chance to hear a range of talented singers and instrumentalists before they become famous.
• Programme from local hotels and libraries.
Phone: 01248 714678
www.beaumarisfestival.co.uk

Cemaes Celtic Festival.
The biennial Cemaes Celtic Festival hosts artists from the other Celtic nations – Ireland, Scotland, the Isle of Man, Cornwall and Brittany – as well as Wales, over the **August** holiday weekend. Run entirely by community volunteers, and supported by local businesses, it provides an important boost to the economy of this attractive harbour village, as well as being an entertaining day out.
• Cemaes is on the north coast of Anglesey, on the A5025.

Holyhead Maritime Festival.
A lively programme of maritime events, both afloat and ashore, including regattas and air-sea rescue displays, brings the crowds to Holyhead's outer harbour each **August.** There are great viewing positions along the promenade at Newry Beach. This is one of the best harbours in the whole of the Irish Sea. Breakwater Park is the place to learn about the construction of the amazing sea wall.
• There is parking along the upper road along Newry Beach and towards the Coastguard Station, or you can walk the modest distance from the town centre.

Island Arts Week. Established by the Anglesey Arts Forum to celebrate the wealth of creative talent to be found on the island, Island Arts Week held each **April** includes workshops, talks, exhibitions, music and dance at venues all over Anglesey. Painters and sculptors open their studios, so that people may see the artists at work, and a wide range of high-quality items is available to buy at the craft fair.
• Details from local art and craft galleries and studios.
Phone: 01407 763361
www.angleseyartsforum.org

Left: **Amlwch Viking Festival.**
This spectacular three-day event includes re-enactments of the Viking raids on Anglesey during the 9th and 10th centuries. Silver ingots, jewellery, household items and coins have been found on the site of a Viking trading settlement at Llanbedrgoch, in eastern Anglesey.

Llandudno, Colwyn Bay, Rhyl and Prestatyn

Great Orme, Llandudno Victorian Trail, Bryn Euryn Iron Age fort, the Alice in Wonderland Centre, the Punch and Judy show, Venue Cymru, Oriel Mostyn Gallery, Theatr Colwyn and Rhyl Pavilion.

Colwyn Bay

Theatr Colwyn. This theatre features a vibrant programme of drama, music, dance and pantomime. The 386-seat auditorium also operates as a cinema.
• Colwyn Bay is served by J21 and J22 on the A55 expressway. Phone: 01492 534263 www.theatrcolwyn.co.uk

Conwy

Conwy Castle. This formidable fortress occupies an excellent defensive position on a rock overlooking the harbour, from which it could be supplied in time of siege. Conwy has the most complete circuit of medieval town walls in the UK, over a kilometre in circumference and guarded by twenty-one towers and three impressive double-towered gateways. Walk around the walls and climb the castle's towers for magnificent views of the harbour in one direction and the mountains of Snowdonia in the other.
• Leave the A55 at J17 or J18. There's a car park next to the castle. Phone: 01492 592358 www.cadw.wales.gov.uk

Above: **Conwy Castle.** Walk around the town walls and you will see that Conwy still has its medieval layout of narrow streets from the quayside to the castle.

Conwy Visitor Centre.

Discover the past and present of this fascinating town through exhibitions and films at the Conwy Visitor Centre in the shadow of the castle. Combine history and fun at the **Brass Rubbing Centre,** and take away an impressive memento.

• A short walk from the castle, towards the town square and High Street.

Phone: 01492 596288

The Smallest House in Britain.

Originally built as a fisherman's cottage, this tiny house is squeezed between larger buildings on Conwy's quayside. Amazingly, its last occupant was six foot three inches (1.9m) tall even though the house only measures nine feet (2.9m) by five feet (1.5m).

• Parking on the quayside, reached via very narrow arches in the town walls, is limited.

Royal Cambrian Academy.

A treat for art enthusiasts and holidaymakers alike, this fine art gallery puts on a varied programme of exhibitions, including ones that tour, throughout the year. The visual delights range from works by academy members, who include some of the most distinguished artists currently working in Wales, to masterpieces by famous painters from the past.

• Just off Conwy's High Street, behind the Elizabethan house Plas Mawr.

Phone: 01492 593413
www.rcaconwy.org

Plas Mawr. At the heart of Conwy's medieval town centre, you will find the finest town house of the Elizabethan era in the UK. The Great Hall was built between 1576 and 1585 for the Welsh merchant Robert Wynn. It has many original furnishings and the decorative plasterwork has been restored to its original splendour. An audio tour describes the restoration of this architectural gem.
• Halfway down the High Street from the town square towards the quayside.
Phone: 01492 580167
www.cadw.wales.gov.uk

Aberconwy House. Dating from the 14th century, this timber-framed merchant's house has survived for more than six centuries. The furnished rooms, described in an audio-visual presentation, show daily life from different periods in its history. Ask about the musical events that are held here from time to time.
• In Castle Street.
Phone: 01492 592246
www.nationaltrust.org.uk

Above: Smallest House in Britain. Tiny indeed in comparison with a conventional house, The Smallest House in Britain was nevertheless acceptable to its fisherman occupant, accustomed perhaps to small cabins at sea.

Conwy suspension bridge.
The elegant suspension bridge between the present road and rail bridges across the river Conwy was designed and built by Thomas Telford and was completed in 1826. It is a pleasant walk across the bridge from the castle.
• Access to the bridge is via the tollhouse at the distant end from the castle.
Phone: 01492 573282
www.nationaltrust.org.uk

Great Ormes Head

The Marine Drive around Great Orme is a masterpiece of Victorian road building, providing panoramic views to Anglesey and Snowdonia. From **Llandudno's promenade**, head past the pier to begin this thrilling five-mile (8km) one way route, as it clings to the cliffs before emerging at the West Shore. It is one of the UK's longest toll roads.
• You can also drive up to the summit of Great Orme from a junction part-way along the Marine Drive. Look out for stray sheep and feral goats.
Phone: 01492 575408
www.visitllandudno.org.uk

Great Orme tramway.
Britain's only cable-hauled public tramway has been operating for more than a century and still uses the original Victorian carriages. The contrast with the cable cars passing high overhead could not be greater. A combined ticket enables you to go up to the summit on one and return on the other.
• The tramway begins at Victoria Station in Church Walk, near the upper end of the main shopping street. The cable cars go from Happy Valley near the pier.
Phone: 01492 879306
www.greatormetramway.co.uk

Great Orme Bronze Age copper mines. This is the oldest metal mine open to the public anywhere in the world. Copper ore was mined here 4,000 years ago during the early Bronze Age, and the site experienced a revival of activity in the eighteenth and nineteenth centuries. You may follow the ancient workings, the earliest of them excavated using bone and stone hand tools, to amazing caverns 150ft (45m) below ground.
• Part-way up the road to Great Ormes summit – parking is limited.
Phone: 01492 870447
www.greatormemines.info

Llandudno

Llandudno Pier and Promenade.
Traditional coastal attractions abound on and around Llandudno's impressive Victorian

Left: Thomas Telford's bridge.
Although built over 500 years apart,
Conwy Castle and Thomas Telford's
bridge over the estuary make a
harmonious pairing.

pier, built so that all could enjoy the views and the therapeutic sea air. There are amusement arcades, along with cafés and bars and a lively programme of entertainment in spring and summer.

• Going to the end of the pier, rather than admiring it from the promenade, really is worthwhile for views of the town and Great Orme.
Phone: 01492 876258
www.visitllandudno.org.uk

Llandudno Victorian Town Trail.
Walking is a great way to explore the generally level town centre and promenade of Llandudno. The town's attractions include the **Victorian Town Trail** (leaflets available from Tourist Information Centres, the library and hotels), the **Home Front Experience,** which re-creates civilian life during the Second World War, and **Llandudno Museum.**
Bus tours of the wider area as far as Conwy start from North Parade near the pier, and are accompanied by a trained guide.

• The fascinating town trail was created primarily for tourists between 1849 and 1912. There are fifteen viewing points marked by information boards.
www.visitllandudno.org.uk

Alice in Wonderland Centre, Llandudno. The real Alice Liddell, who inspired Lewis Carroll to write his enchanting tales of Alice's Adventures in Wonderland, enjoyed summer holidays with her family at their house on Llandudno's West Shore.
At this entertaining town centre attraction you may walk through the magical rabbit hole and into the stories yourself, and experience her adventures through colourful displays and recorded excerpts.

• Located in Trinity Square, off Mostyn Street, just east of the centre of town.
Phone: 01492 860082
www.wonderland.co.uk

Llandudno Museum.
Enjoy exploring the town's fascinating history, from spotting the footprint on a Roman tile, to visiting a traditional Welsh kitchen with its pots and pans, or to examining the many items that bring the town's role as a holiday resort to life. Temporary exhibitions show an ever-changing programme of items from the museum collections and work by local artists.

• In Gloddaeth Street, with parking within walking distance.
Phone: 01492 876517
www.llandudno-tourism.co.uk /museum

Venue Cymru. This 1500-seat theatre, with its associated exhibition spaces and pleasant restaurant, has established itself

Left: **The Great Orme tramway. Provides outstanding views over the wide sweep of Llandudno's North Shore promenade.**

as one of the leading live performance venues in Wales. Its diverse programme ranges from children's shows and pantomime to opera, Welsh music, ballet, rock and pop music, comedy and musical theatre. It also hosts exhibitions, political conferences and the popular **North Wales Country Music Festival.**
• On the promenade, with ample car parking nearby.
Phone: 01492 872000
www.venuecymru.co.uk

Oriel Mostyn Gallery. The Mostyn Art Gallery was established in 1901 by Lady Augusta Mostyn to show the work of the Gwynedd Ladies Art Society, making it the first gallery in the world built specifically for work by female artists. It is now one of the UK's premier contemporary, modern and fine art galleries and displays major exhibitions of Welsh and international art. The craft shop stocks handmade jewellery, ceramics and glassware ranging from the classic to the quirky, along with books, prints and cards.
• Next door to the main Post Office, 200 yards from Llandudno's railway station.
Phone: 01492 879201
www.mostyn.org

The Home Front Experience.
Step back to the time of the Second World War and discover the dangers and difficulties that the civilian population then faced.

The sights and sounds of air raids, rationing, digging for victory, make do and mend, and morale-boosting singalongs are evocatively re-created in displays and tableaux.
• In Llandudno's New Street, behind the church.
Phone: 01492 871032

Professor Codman's Punch and Judy Show. This is the real thing: an authentic performance of the raucous puppet show which, preserved and presented by several generations of the same family, has delighted audiences in Llandudno since the 1860s. The dysfunctional couple and their supporting cast of characters, including the crocodile and the policeman, are here waiting for you to cheer and boo!
• Follow the sounds of laughter amongst the gardens at the pier end of the promenade.
www.punchandjudy.com/codgal.htm

Above left: **Oriel Mostyn Gallery.** Described as 'one of the most adventurous contemporary art venues in the country', Oriel Mostyn Gallery also features temporary exhibitions, educational workshops and events.
Above right: **Llandudno Beach.** The Blue Flag recognises the cleanliness of the beach, and its excellent facilities – there's usually something interesting happening too, from children's entertainment to lifeboat days and bandstand concerts.

Llangernyw

Sir Henry Jones Museum, Llangernyw. This fascinating museum of rural life is the childhood home of Sir Henry Jones (1852-1922) who, from humble origins, went on to become an eminent Professor of Moral Philosophy at Glasgow University and an influential figure in education in Wales.
• The village of Llangernyw is on the A548, between J24 of the A55 and Llanrwst.
Phone: 01492 575571
www.sirhenryjones-museums.org

Rhos-on-Sea

Saint Trillo's chapel, Rhos-on-Sea. After the departure of the Romans, what is now England fell to the Saxons. The Celtic saints who roamed Wales, Scotland and Ireland established their cells, monasteries and churches and kept the flame of Christianity alive. The church of Saint Trillo dates from the 6th century; its altar was built directly over an existing holy well.
• Rhos-on-Sea – Llandrillo-yn-Rhos – is between Llandudno and Colwyn Bay, near J20 on the A55.
www.visitllandudno.org.uk

Harbour at Rhos-on-Sea.
A plaque on an old section of stone wall, said to be the original quayside, claims that it was from here, in the year 1170, that Prince Madog ap Owain Gwynedd sailed westward and discovered America, 322 years before Columbus's voyage. Porthmadog also claims the honour of being his departure port. But strenuous attempts to prove the story, including research into apparent similarities between Welsh and the languages of certain Native American peoples, have proved inconclusive.
• The promenade here is a quiet alternative to the bustle of Llandudno.
www.visitllandudno.org.uk

Rhyl

Pavilion Theatre. With over a thousand seats, this is a large regional performance space, established in 1991 and designed to accommodate all types of theatre and music, together with exhibitions and conferences.
• Rhyl is reached by means of the A525 dual carriageway from J27 on the A55.
Phone: 0870 330 0000
www.pavilion-theatre-rhyl.co.uk

Tal-y-cafn

Bodnant Garden. As you explore its many delights, you will understand why this is described as one of the world's finest gardens. Formal Italianate

Left: **Bodnant Garden.** Offering tremendous contrasts from season to season, and between the formal gardens and the woodland. It rewards repeated visits.

terraces give tremendous views over the Conwy valley to Snowdonia. Spectacular woodland contains the UK's largest giant redwood and many other towering trees. The famous laburnum arch reaches its bright golden-yellow peak in May.
• Off the A470 some five miles south of Conwy.
Phone: 01492 650460
www.bodnant-garden.co.uk

geometric patterns have been produced here for a hundred and fifty years. At the nearby spa, learn about its establishment by the Romans and its popularity in Victorian times, and sample the spa water it still produces today.
• Trefriw is on the B5106 between Betws-y-Coed and Conwy, near Llanrwst.
Phone: 01492 640462
www.t-w-m.co.uk

Trefriw

Trefriw Woollen Mill and Spa.
This working mill generates its own electricity from the rushing waters of the river Crafnant, as it descends to join the river Conwy. Traditional Welsh bedspreads and tweeds with their colourful

Festivals and events

Llandudno Festival of Music and the Arts.
During **July**, Llandudno's streets and entertainment venues offer a wealth of outdoor and indoor activity. There are lunchtime and evening concerts, organised

walks, Welsh folk music and dancing, street entertainers, tea dances on the pier, poetry readings and much more.

• Programmes from libraries, the Venue Cymru Theatre box office and via the Arts Council of Wales website.

Phone: 01492 546506

www.north-wales-events.co.uk

Llandudno Victorian Extravaganza and Transport Festival. The orderly planning of Llandudno's attractive streets and promenade, which set the scene for the town's emergence as the most genteel of Victorian seaside resorts, was instigated in the 1840s by Lord Mostyn, the local landowner and Member of Parliament. The first weekend of **May** each year sees the return of the colourful costumes and traditions of those days.

The **Transport Festival** attracts a large gathering of immaculately turned out classic and vintage vehicles.

• Programmes from Tourist Information Centre.

www.victorian-extravaganza.co.uk

Above left: **Llandudno.** The long tradition of seaside Punch and Judy shows continues in Llandudno. Join the crowds for performances each afternoon, weather permitting, between Easter and mid-September.

Above right: **Llandudno Festival of Music and Art.** This summer extravaganza brings a host of performers and musicians to this popular seaside resort.

North Wales Borderlands

Llangollen, St Winefride's Well, St Asaph Cathedral,
Valle Crucis Abbey, the Pontcysyllte aqueduct, Erddig
Hall, Llangollen International Musical Eisteddfod,
Clwyd Theatr Cymru, Bodelwyddan Castle and
Ruthin Craft Centre.

Bodelwyddan

Church of St Margaret, Bodelwyddan.
The remarkable 'Marble Church' of Bodelwyddan is one of the showiest of all Victorian showpiece churches. The founder of this lavish church was Margaret, daughter of Sir John Williams of Bodelwyddan Castle and widow of Henry Lord Willoughby de Broke. A wealthy and strong-minded woman, she was determined to commemorate her husband by building the finest possible church in the Gothic Revival style, an aim she more than achieved.

• An impressive sight from the A55 between J25 and J26, west of St Asaph.

Phone: 01745 584563
www.bodelwyddan-castle.co.uk

Bodelwyddan Castle – National Portrait Gallery. Set in 260 acres of magnificent parkland, Bodelwyddan Castle is now an outstation of the National Portrait Gallery. The castle as seen today is a creation of Sir John Hay Williams, and dates from between 1830 and 1852, though the estate has medieval origins. Architects Hansom (designer of

Above: **Bodelwyddan Castle.** At Bodelwyddan Castle, in surroundings conducive to the enjoyment of great art, the National Portrait Gallery arranges a changing programme of exhibitions of its many treasures.

the horse-drawn cab) and
Welch were employed by
Sir John to refurbish and extend
the house, while further works
at this time also resulted in a
magnificent estate wall and
formal garden.
• Between J25 and J26 on the
A55 expressway.
Phone: 01745 584060
www.bodelwyddan-castle.co.uk

Chirk

Chirk Castle. Completed in 1310,
Chirk's rather austere exterior
contrasts with the elegant and
comfortable staterooms inside,
with their fine plasterwork,
Adam-style furniture, tapestries
and portraits. The castle, as you
will see from a distance as you

approach and pass through the
ornate gates, is surrounded by
extensive parkland and formal
gardens. After four hundred
years of continuous occupation,
it is still lived in by the
Myddelton family.
• Just inside Wales, off the A5,
some seven miles east of
Llangollen.
Phone: 01691 777701
www.nationaltrust.org.uk

Corwen

Rug Chapel and Llangar Church.
These delightful religious
buildings will take you back
to another age. Rug is a rare
example of a little-altered private
chapel of the 17th century.
Its exterior is plain but inside –

from the pew ends to the amazing roof – the skills of local woodcarvers and artists were given free rein. Llangar Church, in contrast, is a medieval building with 15th century wall paintings and a minstrels' gallery. It was remodelled in the early 18th century.

• Close together near Corwen. Rug is a mile to the north-west on the A494, and Llangar is a mile to the south-west on the B4401.
www.llangollen.com

encircling town walls, was put up by Henry de Lacy, Earl of Lincoln, one of Edward I's commanders during his late-13th century campaigns against the Welsh. There are panoramic views of the Vale of Clwyd from the castle and its ramparts.

• There is parking space at the castle; the lower gatehouse is amid narrow residential streets. Phone: 01745 813385
www.cadw.wales.gov.uk

Denbigh

Denbigh Castle. Crowning the steep hill above the town, Denbigh Castle, along with the mighty gatehouse below and the

Above: **Chirk Castle.** The solid exterior of Chirk Castle contrasts with its appealing parkland setting and with the delightful furnishing and decoration of its rooms.

Theatr Twm o'r Nant, Denbigh.
Community productions, particularly in the Welsh language, are the staple of this thriving theatre in Denbigh. It also hosts public talks and recordings of BBC radio programmes, as well as meetings and rehearsals of local choirs, groups and societies.
Its programme is typical of the ferment of cultural activity that goes on every week throughout Wales.
• Details from Denbigh Library and local bookshops.
Phone: 01745 550374
www.visitdenbigh.co.uk

HM Stanley Exhibition, Denbigh.
Explorer, journalist and author Henry Morton Stanley overcame a harsh childhood as an orphan in Denbigh, to achieve fame and many honours in Britain and the USA. His finest hour came when he fulfiled a commission from the 'New York Herald' to find the Victorian explorer David Livingstone, who was presumed lost in the depths of Africa. When he found him, Stanley uttered the immortal words "Doctor Livingstone, I presume..."
• Items are on display at Denbigh Library and Museum.
www.visitdenbigh.co.uk

Flint

Flint Castle. Built following the Welsh campaigns of Edward I in 1277, Flint is one of his lesser-known castles. Standing solidly on the shore of the Dee estuary, it reflects the importance of secure access to and from the sea, as do many castles around Wales. This is where Richard II was held in 1399 before he was dethroned and replaced as king by Henry IV.
• On the Dee estuary coast between Connah's Quay and Holywell.
www.cadw.wales.gov.uk

Greenfield Valley

Step back in time as you walk through this attractive country park, where birdsong and the scents of wild flowers have replaced the cacophony and noxious fumes of the copper smelting works that once stood here. At the museum and farm, reconstructed buildings contain agricultural displays, a working smithy and farm animals.
• From J32 on the A55, follow signs to Greenfield Valley.
Phone: 01352 714172
www.greenfieldvalley.com

Basingwerk Abbey. Less remote than most other monasteries of the the Cistercian order, the picturesque ruins of 12th century

Left: Basingwerk Abbey. Unlike many medieval abbeys, Basingwerk was within reach of centres of population and the monks there made a good living from the agricultural produce they sold locally.

Basingwerk Abbey are to be found in the **Greenfield Valley Heritage Park**. The monastic community here was renowned for its hospitality to visitors. Traveller and writer Gerald of Wales came here in 1188 and Edward I stayed here whilst building Flint Castle in the 13th century. The monks profited from trading in wool, salt, lead and silver. Pilgrims thronging to nearby St Winefride's Well, which was in the care of the abbey, brought additional prosperity. The abbey was dissolved in 1536 by Henry VIII. Only a little of the 12th century walling survives and much of what is visible today, including the church, dates from the early 13th century when the buildings were generally refurbished and extended. The attractions of the Greenfield Valley make a marvellously varied walk. www.cadw.wales.gov.uk

Hawarden

St Deiniol's Library. Britain's only residential library was founded by the great Victorian statesman and four-times Prime Minister, William Ewart Gladstone. Following his death in 1898, it became the nation's memorial to his life and work. A voracious reader and collector of books, he assembled a remarkable collection reflecting his many interests. This has since grown to more than 200,000 volumes on history, theology, philosophy,

the classics, art and literature.
• St Deiniol's Library is in Hawarden, just north of the A55 at J35, along the A550.
Phone: 01244 532350
www.st-deiniols.co.uk

Holywell

St Winefride's Well. This most famous of all of the holy wells of Wales has been in continuous use as a place of healing since medieval times. King Henry V walked here from Shrewsbury, to give thanks for victory at Agincourt. The elaborate vaulted chapel over the well was built in around 1500, at the instigation of Margaret Beaufort, mother of Henry VII. King James II and his wife Mary came here in 1686 to pray, successfully, for a son. The beautiful statue of St Winefride and the calm environs of the shrine and the nearby church enhance the deep spiritual significance of this remarkable place, where pilgrims still come to bathe in the healing waters.
• Down the hill from Holywell town centre. There is a car park at a respectful distance, from which it is but a short walk to the well.
Phone: 01352 713054
www.saintwinefrideswell.com

Above: **Llangollen Canal.** Relaxing horse-drawn boat trips along the scenic Llangollen Canal offer great views over the town and to the surrounding hills.

Pantasaph Friary.

This Franciscan friary welcomes visitors who are keen to learn more about Catholic spirituality. It is home to the national shrine of St Pio, operates as a retreat centre and offers an uplifting walk around an outdoor representation of the Stations of the Cross.
• Immediately west of Holywell – accessible from J31 and J32 of the A55.

....

Llangollen

Few towns anywhere enjoy a more picturesque location. Framed by green hills, one of them topped by the ruins of **Castell Dinas Brân,** and with the river Dee rushing under its fine stone bridge, the town is a delightful place to explore.
• From the several car parks, follow the comprehensively signed walking routes along the river bank and around the town. www.borderlands.co.uk For details of Llangollen International Musical Eisteddfod see page 65.

Llangollen Canal. This is generally agreed among canal-cruising folk to be the most beautiful canal in the UK. It extends some forty miles westward from the Shropshire Union canal, which is a pleasant three-day cruise for a narrowboat, and enters Wales in the most spectacular fashion possible, crossing high above the

Dee valley on the **Chirk and Pontcysyllte aqueducts**.
• There are horse-drawn boat trips if you would like a brief introduction to the canal's delights.
www.waterscape.com

Llangollen Steam Railway.
This scenic section of the Ruabon to Barmouth railway line closed to passengers in 1965 and to goods in 1968, when the tracks and signalling were removed. A keen group of volunteers has since reinstated several miles of track along the **Dee valley** towards Corwen. Trains operate at weekends for most of the year, and daily from June to October. It is a joy to hear the tooting of the trains and to savour the atmosphere of the old station as sunlight slants through the smoke and steam. Regular events include **steam galas** with visiting engines, appearances by Thomas the Tank Engine, and Santa Specials.
• The station is just across the bridge from the town centre.
www.llangollen-railway.co.uk

Llangollen Motor Museum.
Take a trip down memory lane to see the cars and motorbikes that your grandparents' generation

Above: **Llangollen Steam Railway. This is the spectacular point where the Llangollen Steam Railway runs high above the river Dee, west of the town, opposite the Chain Bridge Hotel.**

used to drive. Remember – or perhaps encounter for the first time – double de-clutching, starting handles, semaphore indicators and the evocative smell of old leather upholstery. See how the village mechanic and his wife lived and worked, and the tools he used. History is fun at Llangollen Motor Museum, and the shop has gifts, books and even some spare parts for older cars.

• Between the canal and the river, just over a mile westward from the bridge towards the Horseshoe Pass.
Phone: 01978 860324
www.llangollenmotormuseum.co.uk

The Chapel – Y Capel Art Gallery.
Conveniently situated near the centre of Llangollen, this gallery in a former chapel aims high, and features changing exhibitions of paintings, prints and ceramics, ranging from landscape to abstract work, by some of the leading artists of Wales.
• Phone: 01978 860828

Castell Dinas Brân. A vigorous walk up the well-marked path from Llangollen to the ruins of Castell Dinas Brân brings wonderful rewards in the form of 360 degree panoramas of the town, the **Dee valley**, **Eglwyseg Mountain** and the **Horseshoe Pass.** Occupied by its original Welsh builders for only a few decades, the castle was attacked by the forces of Edward I in 1277 and has remained in ruins ever

since. Wordsworth was moved to lament its fate with the words: 'Relic of kings, wreck of forgotten wars. To the winds abandoned and the prying stars.'
• The Tourist Information Centre and local shops have maps and guidebooks describing walks and cycle routes.
Phone: 01352 810614
www.denbighshire.gov.uk

Plas Newydd. This timbered mansion was home to the Ladies of Llangollen – the Irish aristocrats Eleanor Butler and Sarah Ponsonby – who settled here and entertained countless society and literary figures during the early decades of the 19th century. Plas Newydd is set in peaceful gardens surrounded by trees and contains the font from the nearby Valle Crucis Abbey. The house is now a museum run by Denbighshire County Council. The circle of stones in the grounds of Plas Newydd were used for the 1908 Llangollen National Eisteddfod.
• Walk up the main street, away from the river, and carefully cross the A5 at the top; head left, then right up a residential road, to nearby Plas Newydd.
Phone: 01978 861314
www.borderlands.co.uk

Above: **Plas Newydd.** William Wordsworth, Sir Walter Scott and the Duke of Wellington were among the luminaries who visited the Ladies of Llangollen at their Gothically furnished and decorated home, Plas Newydd.

Valle Crucis Abbey. One of the most attractively situated of Wales's sacred places, Valle Crucis takes its name – Vale of the Cross – from the beautiful valley near Llangollen where a 9th century cross, the Pillar of Eliseg, stands. Founded in 1201 by the local Welsh ruler, Madoc ap Gruffydd Maelor, whose family later built the hilltop fortress of **Dinas Brân**, the abbey conformed to the rules of the white-robed Cistercians, which stated that their monasteries should be built "far from the haunts of men".
• Between Llangollen and the spectacular Horseshoe Pass, on the A542.
www.cadw.wales.gov.uk

Mold

This pleasing market town is the birthplace of Daniel Owen, one of the finest novelists in the Welsh language. The museum above the library chronicles his life and introduces the much-loved characters in his late 19th century novels. The compact town centre has family-run shops among familiar high street names. The bustling street market, popular since the 17th century, extends from the square towards the parish church every Wednesday and Saturday.
• Signed from the A55 and from Wrexham.
www.borderlands.co.uk

Clwyd Theatr Cymru. This highly acclaimed centre of theatrical excellence, standing on the hill above Mold, is home to Wales's major drama-producing theatre company. Under the inspired leadership of director Terry Hands, the actors and technicians achieve production standards that are second to none. The company regularly presents its work on tour throughout Wales, and the theatre also hosts visiting productions, concerts, and exhibitions.
• Drive up past the council offices to the car parks in front of the theatre.
Phone: 01352 756331
www.clwyd-theatr-cymru.co.uk

Rhuddlan

This was yet another of the castles built by Edward I. He issued the Statute of Rhuddlan here in 1284, imposing English legal and administrative systems on the territories he had seized. The castle's most remarkable attribute is the means by which ships were able to bring supplies to its river gate, some three miles from the sea. In a mammoth exercise involving hundreds of workers, the River Clwyd was deepened and straightened to make a canal.

Right: **Valle Crucis Abbey.** A short distance north of Llangollen, on the way to the dramatic Horseshoe Pass, Valle Crucis Abbey graces a sylvan valley of great beauty.

• A couple of miles north of St Asaph, from J27 on the A55 expressway.
Phone: 01745 590777
www.cadw.wales.gov.uk

Ruthin

There are some remarkable listed buildings around the town square of Ruthin. Several of the half-timbered buildings, now occupied by banks and shops, have been in business since medieval times.
St Peter's Church was the first to be built in the spacious double-naved style found in this part of the UK. Look for the "Eyes of Ruthin", the distinctive dormer windows in the roof of the **Castle Hotel** on the square.
• All approaches give wide views of the broad Vale of Clwyd.
www.borderlands.co.uk

Ruthin Castle. A succession of owners since medieval times enlarged this fortified site. In 1826, a fine house was built over part of the castle and was later extended. Ruthin Castle is now a hotel and conference centre; it has become famous for its medieval-style Welsh banquets, with traditional food, drink and entertainment.
• A short drive or walk along a narrow road leading from the main town square.
Phone: 01824 702664
www.ruthincastle.co.uk

Ruthin Gaol. The stout walls and barred windows of Ruthin Gaol

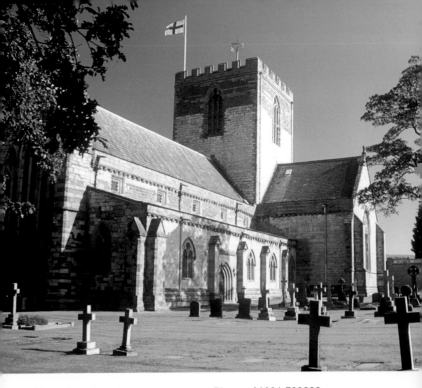

still exude a daunting presence, though you may visit nowadays and tour the interior, including the condemned man's cell, with the certainty of getting out again.
• A short walk down the hill from Ruthin's ancient main square.

Ruthin Craft Centre.
This purpose-built craft centre has two exhibition galleries displaying a changing programme of contemporary applied art. There is a shop and a pleasant restaurant, as well as independent workshops accommodating designer-craftworkers whose activities include glass blowing, ceramics, textiles, fine art prints and jewellery.
• On the edge of the town centre, with parking available.

Phone: 01824 703992
www.borderlands.co.uk

. . . .

St Asaph

St Asaph Cathedral. This is the mother church of the diocese of St Asaph, one of the six dioceses of the Church in Wales. The Celtic saint Kentigern built his original church here in 560 AD. When he returned to Strathclyde in 573 AD

Above left: **Mold.** The town centre of Mold is busy with activity during the traditional Wednesday and Saturday street markets which have been held since 1808.
Above right: **St Asaph Cathedral.** Destroyed by the armies of Henry III in 1245 and Edward I in 1282, St Asaph Cathedral was substantially rebuilt only to be burned by Owain Glyndŵr's Welsh troops in 1402.

59

he left Asaph as his successor, and the cathedral has been dedicated to St Asaph since that time. The present building was begun in the 13th century and is generally agreed to be the smallest cathedral in the UK. Its bishops have included the Norman writer and historian Geoffrey of Monmouth and Bishop William Morgan, who translated the Bible into Welsh.
• Within sight of the A55 – exit at J27.
Phone: 01745 583429
www.stasaphcathedral.org.uk

....

Trelawnyd

Gop cairn at Trelawnyd.
The enormous mound on Gop Hill is the biggest prehistoric monument in Wales and the second largest in all Britain, outmatched only by Silbury Hill near Avebury. Standing 46 feet (14m) tall, and some 820 feet (250m) above sea level, the limestone blocks used to build the great oval mound are plain to see. It is usually given a late-Neolithic origin, somewhere around 3,000 BC, but the purpose for which it was so laboriously built is shrouded in mystery. As with similar monuments, possibilities include an astronomical viewing platform, a focus for rituals connected with sun worship, a monument to the dead, or a massive burial mound.
• Five miles eastward from Rhuddlan, on the A5151.

Wrexham

As the largest town in north Wales, Wrexham is a busy commercial and administrative centre with all of the educational, cultural, sports and leisure resources you would expect. Its origins as a market town are preserved in the half-timbered building of the town centre and the three excellent indoor markets.

• The town centre is pedestrianised and suitably compact for exploration on foot. www.wrexham.gov.uk

Wrexham Arts Centre.
The Centre has two galleries, organises touring exhibitions and is a popular venue for art classes, lectures and school visits. In association with the **Yale Memorial Gallery** – at Yale College – it has organised, exhibited and toured successful international print exhibitions. **The Regional Print Centre** provides print-making facilities to artists and the public, for monotype, etching, relief and screenprinting on paper, textiles, ceramics and glass.

• If you are unfamiliar with this largest of north-Wales towns, a detailed map or visitor guide will

Above: **Erddig Hall.** Elaborate 18th century gardens and sumptuous interiors are testimony to the no-expense-spared approach to materials and workmanship at this fine country house.

come in handy.
Phone: 01978 292093
(Arts Centre)
Phone: 01978 311794
(Gallery/Print Centre)

Erddig Hall. Here, in one of the most fascinating historic houses in the UK, you will experience something of the intertwined lives of a family and its servants. The former occupied the outstandingly beautiful staterooms, with their fine 18th and 19th century furniture and decor, including some exquisite Chinese wallpaper. The latter worked away in the kitchen, bakehouse, laundry, stables, smithy and sawmill. The large walled garden has been restored to its formal 18th century glory and contains the national collection of ivy varieties.
• Prominently signed from the main approaches to Wrexham from the south.
Phone: 01978 355314
www.nationaltrust.org.uk

St Giles's Church. The massive tower of St Giles's Wrexham dominates the town's skyline and is justly numbered among the "Seven Wonders of Wales". Richly decorated and pinnacled, it stands 147 feet (45 metres) high. It has a twin across the Atlantic – a replica built in the 1920s at Yale University to honour that institution's benefactor, Elihu Yale of Wrexham, who lies buried only a few feet from St Giles's tower.
• There is a large car park

immediately below the elevated site of the church.
Phone: 01978 355808
www.wrexham.gov.uk

Gallery 103 at NEWI. The North East Wales Institute of Higher Education, part of the University of Wales, opened its Gallery 103 in 2002. It quickly proved an asset to the local community, displaying works by a wide range of internationally famous artists, along with the work of NEWI's art students, in exhibitions that change throughout the year.
The William Aston Hall, also part of NEWI, accommodates musical performances and public lectures.
Phone: 01978 290666
www.newi.ac.uk

Clywedog Valley.
Wrexham's industrial heritage is dramatically preserved at the **Bersham Heritage Centre Iron Works** and **Minera Lead Mines**. Follow the fascinating Clywedog Valley trail and call at the **Nant Mill Visitor Centre** to learn about the area's contribution to the Industrial Revolution.
• Five miles west of Wrexham on the A525, or carefully navigate

Right: **Llangollen International Musical Eisteddfod.** Hundreds of colourfully costumed competitors travel from all over the world to enjoy the camaraderie and high performance standards of the Llangollen International Musical Eisteddfod.

the remote and narrow mountain road from Llangollen via World's End.
Phone: 01978 261529 (Bersham Heritage Centre) Phone: 01978 752772 (Nant Mill Visitor Centre)
www.wrexham.gov.uk

Rhosllanerchrugog Miners' Institute. Culture and education were given high priority in the mining and quarrying communities of Wales. Institutes such as this housed the theatres, meeting rooms and libraries in which the miners and their families elevated their thoughts from the harshness of the pit. The Stiwt, restored to its considerable former glory, combines a state-of-the-art theatre with a multi-purpose

Welsh cultural centre, befitting its place at the heart of a talented community with deep and long-standing cultural traditions.
• Often described as Wales's largest village, Rhosllanerchrugog is on the B5097 south-west of Wrexham.
Phone: 01978 844053
www.stiwt.co.uk

Festivals and events

Flintshire Festival. October is the time to enjoy this well-established mix of music, dance and drama, along with interesting guided walks and talks during which you will learn about the history and culture of this north-eastern corner of Wales.
www.flintshire.gov.uk

Gŵyl Cadi Ha – folk dancing.
Traditional Welsh folk dancing
ranges from the athletic clog
dances enjoyed by off-duty farm
workers in centuries past to the
sedate formations practised by
the gentry in the grand houses.
The colourful costumes and
precision steps are revived at
this celebration at the beginning
of **May**, led by the mischievous
figure of Cadi Ha' and echoing
seasonal celebrations dating
back to pagan times.
• A roving event in the vicinity of
Holywell, the Greenfield Valley
and Mold.
Phone: 01352 755614

**Llangollen International Musical
Eisteddfod.** This wonderful
celebration of diverse cultures
was founded as a means of
bringing nations together and
healing the scars left by the
Second World War. Musicians and
dancers from all over the world
travel to Llangollen in early
July to enjoy the atmosphere
of friendly competition and the
warm welcome extended by the

Above left: **Llangollen Eisteddfod.**
Welsh and Chinese dragons met
when this troupe of Hakka Chinese
dancers visited the Llangollen
Eisteddfod, which was founded over
sixty years ago.
Above right: **Llangollen Eisteddfod.**
These Lithuanian musicians
attending the Llangollen Eisteddfod
went out and about to perform on
the square in Ruthin, also a popular
venue for events during the Ruthin
Festival.

town. Evening concerts feature big names from classical music, opera, world music and musical theatre.

• The Llangollen International Pavilion is within walking distance of the town centre, across the bridge and to the left. Phone: 01978 862000 www.international-eisteddfod.co.uk

North Wales International Jazz Guitar Festival. The organisers reckon, with considerable justification, that this is the biggest and most exciting event of its kind in the world. It features the cream of jazz guitarists from the UK and the rest of Europe, along with visiting luminaries from the USA.

• Held in **August** at venues in and around Wrexham. Phone: 01745 812260 www.northwalesjazz.org.uk

North Wales International Music Festival. The attractive cathedral of St Asaph is the main venue for this festival held every **September**. Orchestral, choral and chamber music is performed by musicians of the highest calibre. The festival is a legacy of the eminent Welsh composer William Mathias, who is buried in the shade of the cathedral and its surrounding trees.

• Programme from local libraries and Tourist Information Centres, or link from the Arts Council of Wales website. Phone: 01745 584508 www.northwalesmusicfestival.co.uk

Denbigh Midsummer Festival.

This week long festival of music, drama, exhibitions and poetry is held in mid **June** in this historic town in the beautiful Vale of Clwyd, which has performance venues of great character.
• Details from Denbigh Library, local shops and hotels.
Phone: 01745 814646
www.visitdenbigh.co.uk

Wrexham Arts Festival

Over sixteen days in **May** and June this exciting festival features classical music, including lunchtime recitals, jazz concerts and dance events. Especially popular are the days devoted specifically to childern's art, literature, music and drama. The Arts Festival takes place at various venues around Wrexham.

• Details are available at the TIC in Wrexham.
Phone: 01978 292015

Ruthin Festival

This varied festival of music, dance and drama is held over a week at the end of **June**. It features interesting guided walks and talks during which you will learn about the history and culture of this north-eastern corner of Wales.
• Details and tickets can be obtained from Ruthin Library.
Phone: 01824 702703
www.ruthinfestival.co.uk

Above: **Ruthin Festival.** The festival is a community event celebrating the best music and culture in a week-long event.

Snowdonia Mountains and Coast

Caernarfon Castle, Tŷ Mawr Wybrnant, Llanrwst, several narrow-gauge railways, Bardsey Island and Portmeirion. The National Slate Museum, Nant Gwrtheyrn, and Bryn Terfel's Faenol Festival are cultural treasures.

Bangor

Penrhyn Castle. In an ostentatious display of the wealth he and his family had extracted from their slate quarries at Bethesda, George Dawkins (who adopted the family name Pennant) built this grandiose mock-Norman mansion near Port Penrhyn, the harbour from which the slate was exported. Queen Victoria famously declined to sleep in the giant slate four-poster bed made especially for her visit to the area.
• Just outside Bangor – leave the A55 at J11 or J12.
Phone: 01248 353084
www.nationaltrust.org.uk

Bardsey Island

The holy island of Bardsey exudes a mystical presence among the racing tides off the tip of the Llŷn peninsula. The tower of the 13th century **St Mary's Abbey**, which was the goal of countless medieval pilgrims, remains standing amid the ruins of the Augustinian monastery.
Merlin the Magician – Myrddin

Above: **Snowdon Horseshoe.** Wales's highest mountain might appear to be pristine wilderness but hill farmers, slate quarrymen and copper miners have all earned a living on its slopes – and a small hydro-electric power station puts the high rainfall generated by the mountain to productive use.

Emrys, to give him his Welsh name – is said to be buried there, along with 20,000 saints. Visits are regulated by the Bardsey Island Trust. Many people each year find that a day spent there, or a longer retreat, can be a spiritually uplifting experience.
• There are spectacular vistas of Bardsey from the minor roads above Aberdaron.

Pilgrim's Route to Bardsey.
By means of arcane spiritual arithmetic, the medieval Catholic Church calculated that three pilgrimages to the holy island of Bardsey equalled one to Rome. But it was not an easy option: the pilgrims had to make their way to the far-western tip of the Llŷn peninsula, then endure the two mile crossing of the often turbulent sea. An early glimmer of a tourism industry catered for their needs, providing accommodation and food, and water from wells on the way.
• Enquire at local Tourist Information Centres or churches for a map to enable you to follow their route.

Beddgelert

Sygun Copper Mine.
Snowdonia is riddled with mine workings: gold, silver, lead, copper and other minerals have been found here over the centuries. Sygun's mine galleries extend deep into the mountain, and an audio commentary describes the lives of the miners. The **Red**

Dragon Heritage Centre tells how the Welsh flag was inspired by the legend of the red dragon of Wales defeating the white dragon of the Saxons in the presence of Merlin the Magician, a defeat that occurred at Dinas Emrys, the rocky outcrop across the valley.
• North-east of Beddgelert, on the A498 towards Capel Curig.
Phone: 01766 890595
www.syguncoppermine.co.uk

Betws-y-coed

Dolwyddelan Castle.
This sentinel, deep in the heart of Snowdonia, is one of several castles built by Llywelyn the Great. The stark square tower, visible for miles around, guarded the strategic pass linking Meirionydd in the south of his kingdom and Conwy in the north. The mildly strenuous walk up to the castle from the car park is very worthwhile for the panoramic mountain vistas.
• Between Betws-y-coed and Blaenau Ffestiniog, on the A470.
Phone: 01690 750366
www.cadw.wales.gov.uk

Above left: **Cwm Croesor.** Thousands of workers once laboured in the slate quarries and mines of Bethesda, Llanberis, Blaenau Ffestiniog and Corris. Above right: **Sygun Copper Mine.** Visitors can discover for themselves the wonders of Sygun - the winding tunnels, large chambers, magnificent stalactites and stalagmites and copper ore veins - just as it was when it was abandoned in 1903.

Tŷ Mawr Wybrnant. Small but significant, this is the birthplace of Bishop William Morgan who, in 1588, translated the Bible into Welsh. By doing so, he made the hearing and reading of exemplary Welsh accessible to all, thus securing the status and future of the language. This National Trust property, in the beautiful and secluded **Wybrnant valley** near Penmachno, has been restored to its likely appearance in the 16th century. A woodland walk takes you past traditionally managed fields, where William Morgan's family once farmed.
• Signed from the A5 just south-east of Betws-y-coed, along the B4406 to Penmachno.
Phone: 01690 760213
www.nationaltrust.org.uk

Blaenau Ffestiniog

Llechwedd Slate Caverns. For a thought-provoking insight into the harsh life of the quarrymen, take the underground train journey at Llechwedd to see where they spent their long working days. We are privileged to be able to enjoy the beautiful rock formations and underground lakes of this deep slate mine without the noise, dust and danger that was involved in extracting the slate and bringing it to the surface.
• Just north of Blaenau Ffestiniog on the A470.
Phone: 01766 830306
www.llechwedd-slate-caverns.co.uk

Caernarfon

The castle is just one of many attractions in Caernarfon, the county town of Gwynedd. Substantial Victorian buildings, including the imposing **County Hall** and the **Harbour Office** on the quay, lend their purposeful presence. The sympathetic architecture of **Gwynedd Council's** modern headquarters sits comfortably amongst the narrow streets in the shadow of the castle. A dynamic sculpture of David Lloyd George appears to be giving a rousing speech over Y Maes, the central square. The steam trains of the **Welsh Highland Railway** head into Snowdonia from the Slate Quay.

• Enjoy exploring the historic streets on foot, and revive yourself at one of the numerous cafés.

Caernarfon – Victoria Dock. The maritime museum at Victoria Dock tells the story of this fascinating port, including its growth during the 19th century as it became an important centre for the export of slate quarried in the mountains. On the quayside is **Galeri**, Caernarfon's thriving arts centre, with its excellent performance spaces complemented by offices and

Above: **Caernarfon Castle.** The imposing scale of Caernarfon Castle is evident from the river Seiont quayside, or from the other side of the River, across the footbridge.

rehearsal rooms for numerous arts organisations. **Gwynedd's county archives**, which contain a treasure trove of historical material, are nearby.

• Just outside the town walls, with limited parking near the museum and ample parking (and a pleasant café) at Galeri.

Caernarfon Castle. The largest of the castles built by Edward I in his attempt to control this corner of Wales dominates the town that has grown around it. It stands at the confluence of the River Seiont and the Menai Strait, near the **Roman fort of Segontium**. Its polygonal towers and contrasting bands of masonry imitate the walls of Constantinople. It echoes the legendary dream of the Roman general Magnus Maximus, defender of north-western Britannia, who saw a vision of a beautiful woman in a distant castle and was said to have found her here. Edward knowingly played on these associations when, in his determination to show his strength, he built this overwhelming symbol of his power.

• From the large car park on the quay, walk around to the entrance at the inland side of the castle. Phone: 01286 677617 www.cadw.wales.gov.uk

Roman fort – Segontium. This base for a regiment of around a thousand infantry, which also served as an administrative centre for the collection of taxes, was founded by Agricola in 77 AD, after he had finally conquered the local Celtic tribe, the Ordovices. The on-site museum has impressive finds from the extensive archaeological excavations that revealed the fort, barracks and stores, and the adjacent temple of Mithras.

• At the edge of town, on the A4085 towards Beddgelert. Phone: 01286 675625 www.segontium.org.uk

Inigo Jones Slate Works. Slate, which varies in colour from bluish-purple to grey or green, is a wonderfully versatile resource. It is a multi-purpose building material, usable in thin layers for roofing and cladding, and in greater bulk for walls and paths. It can resist all that the weather might throw at it and lasts for many centuries. It is also capable of being intricately shaped into jewellery and decorative items, and is used, finely ground, in cosmetics. Here, at one of the region's smaller slate quarries, you will find a workshop producing a wide range of attractive items, both functional and artistic.

• Off the A487, some five miles south of Caernarfon. Phone: 01286 830242 www.inigojones.co.uk

Right: Llechwedd Slate Caverns. You will be lent hard hats for your exciting rail journey deep underground.

Corris

King Arthur's Labyrinth, Corris.
Wales has many sites associated
with King Arthur, whose legends
are likely to have grown from the
real-life exploits of a Celtic
chieftain (or perhaps several of
them) who emerged after the
departure of the Romans.
The tales are re-told in dramatic
underground settings at
King Arthur's Labyrinth near
Corris in southern Snowdonia.
• Between Dolgellau and
Machynlleth, on the A487.
Phone: 01654 761584
www.kingarthurslabyrinth.com

Criccieth

Criccieth Castle. Originally a
stronghold of the Welsh princes
with a gatehouse built by
Llywelyn the Great between 1230
and 1240, Criccieth Castle fell to
Edward I in 1283. It was captured
and burned by Owain Glyndŵr
in 1404. The walls still bear
evidence of scorching from that
attack. Dramatically situated on
a headland between two beaches,
it has inspired countless artists,
including JMW Turner.
• Head westward from
Porthmadog towards Pwllheli
(A497). Your first sighting of the
castle guarding the bay will be
memorable.
Phone: 01766 522227
www.cadw.wales.gov.uk

Harlech

Harlech Castle. With the sea on one side of its cliff-top location, the tough terrain of Snowdonia on the other, and a massive gatehouse guarding its landward side, Harlech Castle would have been a tough nut to crack for any attacker. Built in the late 13th century, as Edward I's stronghold in southern Gwynedd, it was occupied by Welsh revolutionary Owain Glyndŵr in 1404. A long siege there during the Wars of the Roses inspired the stirring song "Men of Harlech".

• From Porthmadog, a small toll to use the minor road across the estuary saves several miles of driving.

Phone: 01766 780552
www.cadw.wales.gov.uk

Llanberis

Dolbadarn Castle. Presiding over Llyn Padarn, at the foot of Snowdon, this is one of the most magnificently situated castles built by the Welsh princes. It guarded the approach to the highest pass through Snowdonia, linking Caernarfon and the

---

Above left: **King Arthur's Labyrinth.** Situated in the former workings of the Braich Goch Slate Mines. Take a boat along the subterranean river, through the great waterfall into the Labyrinth and back in time.
Above right: **Harlech Castle.** Almost four centuries after it was built, this mighty castle was the very last Royalist stronghold to fall (in 1647) at the end of the first Civil War.

Conwy valley. It has been a popular subject for landscape painters since the pioneering visits by the great Welsh artist Richard Wilson. Several atmospheric studies were produced here, in both oils and watercolour, by JMW Turner, one of which he submitted as his Diploma work to the Royal Academy.

• There is a car park just along the road to the National Slate Museum, and a footpath leads through woodland to the castle. www.cadw.wales.gov.uk

National Slate Museum.
Llanberis was a major centre of the slate-quarrying industry that once employed thousands in this corner of Wales. The tough working conditions and the camaraderie of the quarry community are brought to life in the original working buildings and terraced cottages preserved at the National Slate Museum, a National Museum Wales site. Former quarrymen demonstrate the skills required to split and trim this remarkable layered rock to make roofing slates and decorative items.

• Off the A4086 at Llanberis. Phone: 01286 870630 www.museumwales.ac.uk

Llanrwst

With its historic centre little changed for four hundred years, this attractive market town serves the surrounding Conwy valley. The hump-backed stone bridge (take care as you cross) was reputedly designed by the famous landscape architect Inigo Jones and dates from 1636. **The Almshouses**, built in 1610, are now a community museum, with an attractive herb garden. Llanrwst considers itself independent of the UK and has its own flag and arms. It once applied (unsuccessfully) for membership of the United Nations!

• Ten miles south of the A55 (J19) and five miles north of Betws-y-coed, on the A470.

Gwydir Castle. Built for the Wynn family in around 1500, this handsome Tudor courtyard house, with peacocks strutting around the Grade I listed formal gardens, has been skilfully restored by its owners. Their efforts included retrieving

Above: **Slate quarrymen.** Evidently proud to be photographed amongst the buildings that today house the National Slate Museum, these quarrymen would find further respite from their dangerous and health-damaging work in the Caban, the canteen where they held classes and discussions on literary and religious topics.

panelling and carvings that had been removed and taken elsewhere – in the case of the panelled dining room from the 1640s, to New York's Metropolitan Museum. Gwydir has a reputation for being one of the most haunted houses in Wales.

• A short drive or a pleasant walk to the opposite side of the River Conwy from Llanrwst.
Phone: 01492 641687
www.gwydircastle.co.uk

Nant Gwrtheyrn

The isolated coastal quarry village of Nant Gwrtheyrn, reached by descending one of the steepest roads in Wales, is now the popular **Welsh Language and Heritage Centre**. In this inspirational location, many people each year learn to speak Welsh on five-day or twelve-day residential courses, or explore Wales's fascinating history. It is also a great place for a brief visit, perhaps including a meal at the restaurant, or a self-catering holiday.

• Follow signs from Llithfaen, on the B4417 north-east of Nefyn – and take great care descending the hill.
Phone: 01758 750334
www.nantgwrtheyrn.org

Portmeirion

Architect Sir Clough Williams-Ellis described his wonderfully eclectic fantasy village as his "Home for Fallen Buildings".

This cornucopia of piazzas, colonnades, domes and arches, enlivened by a riot of fountains, ornate gateways, belvederes, statues and flower borders, depends for its effect on his gift for arranging vistas, perspective and focal points into a most pleasing whole. Portmeirion is generally Italian in style, though there are numerous buildings and features saved from demolition in Wales and elsewhere. Fans of the television series The Prisoner visit to see where their hero tried so hard to escape from the Village. The **Portmeirion** and **Castell Deudraeth hotels**, both within the estate, are great places to stay or to enjoy a meal.

• Prominently signed at Minffordd, between Porthmadog and Penrhyndeudraeth to the east.
Phone: 01766 770228
www.portmeirion-village.com

Rhiw

Plas yn Rhiw. This small 16th century manor house, which has Georgian additions, was rescued from neglect and lovingly restored by the three Keating sisters, who bought it in 1938. The views of Cardigan Bay are spectacular. The delightful ornamental garden has box hedges and grass paths, and is

Left: **Gwydir Castle.**
Restored interiors will take you back some five centuries, to the time of Henry VIII.

81

a riot of flowering trees and shrubs in summer.

• Carefully negotiate the minor roads between Abersoch and Aberdaron at the extremity of the Llŷn peninsula.
Phone: 01758 780219
www.nationaltrust.org.uk

Tre'r Ceiri

Iron Age fort at Tre'r Ceiri.
The Celtic people who lived in Britain before the arrival of the Romans usually built their settlements on easily defended hilltops or narrow coastal promontories. Tre'r Ceiri – Town of the Giants – occupies a spectacular position crowning one of the sharp peaks of The Rivals, with uninterrupted views in all directions.
A three-metre-high wall surrounds some 150 stone hut bases, making this a community of considerable size.

• Close to Llanaelhaearn, fourteen miles south-west of Caernarfon on the A499.
The climb to Tre'r Ceiri is strenuous.

Tywyn

Castell y Bere. The southernmost of the castles of the kingdom of Gwynedd stands near the border with Ceredigion on a rocky outcrop on the floor of the Dysynni valley, where a well provided fresh water. The layout of the interior, including the royal apartments, is clearly preserved, and it is easy to imagine Prince Llywelyn the Great, who built it, enjoying peaceful times here with his family and court.

• The B4405 and the Talyllyn narrow-gauge railway head up the Dysynni valley from Tywyn to Abergynolwyn. A minor road leads to the castle.
www.cadw.wales.gov.uk

Railways. Nothing quite matches the atmosphere of a trip on a steam train as it rattles over the points and chuffs along through the countryside, the experience intensified by that evocative bouquet of smoke, soot and hot oil. The **Ffestiniog, Welsh Highland, Snowdon, Padarn Lake, Talyllyn** and **Bala Lake railways** provide an escape from the car and a great way of enjoying the view. Some lines have industrial origins: the **Ffestiniog Railway** was built to bring slate down from the quarries to ships at Porthmadog. Others are purely scenic: the **Snowdon Railway** has carried passengers to the summit of Wales's highest mountain since 1896.

• Timetables and details from Tourist Information Centres.
www.visitwales.com

Left: **Portmeirion.**
Pleasingly composed vistas – through arches, between buildings, along lanes and across the colourful gardens – appear at every turn as you wander the delightful grounds.

Festivals and events

Abersoch Jazz Festival.
The seaside village of Abersoch echoes to the sounds of jazz, including both indoor and outdoor performances, during early **June** each year. Famous names and local musicians; street music and a colourful parade; competitions, stalls and a gospel music service all maintain the international flavour of this popular festival.
• For Abersoch, follow the A497 and A499 from Porthmadog and Pwllheli.
www.abersochjazzfestival.com

Bryn Terfel's Faenol Festival.
When the internationally renowned bass-baritone Bryn Terfel, who was born in Snowdonia and now lives near Caernarfon, decided to give something back to the community that nurtured his outstanding musical abilities, he did not do so half-heartedly. Each year, he invites some of the biggest stars of opera, musical theatre, rock and Welsh popular music to join him on stage at his four-day festival. This musical feast of the highest order, held over the **August** bank-holiday weekend, enjoys a spectacular location at the Faenol Estate near Bangor, with Snowdonia as a backdrop, and has been voted the Best Show in Wales.

• The Faenol Estate is just west of Bangor, close to J9 on the A55 expressway.
Phone: 01286 672232 (TIC)
www.brynfest.com

Criccieth Festival. Mid **June** finds this most picturesque of seaside towns buzzing with musical and literary activity. Classical musicians, Welsh choirs, singers and dancers, and visiting performers from overseas bring a wonderful variety of styles to the town's fine Memorial Hall and other venues.
Other highlights include fascinating talks, including the **David Lloyd George Memorial Lecture**, garden visits and a family fun day with fireworks.
• Criccieth is on the A497 and is also well served by train services between Porthmadog and Pwllheli.
Phone: 01766 522778
www.cricciethfestival.co.uk

Gwyl Bwyd Môr Llŷn Seafood Festival. This annual seafood festival promises to be 'an assault on the tastebuds'. Held at Pwllheli Marina over a weekend in early **July**, it displays the culinary riches of the sea as well as other locally produced Welsh foods. The festival involves tastings, cookery demonstrations and lectures where visitors can learn about the art of cooking seafood from celebrity chefs. The festival is organised by the Llŷn Fishermen's Association.

• Pwllheli is just off the A499 and is also served by regular trains.
Phone: 01758 720656

Sesiwn Fawr Dolgellau.
The "Big Session" in **July** has outgrown its former home on the town square. Nowadays its five main stages occupy the Marian, the area of car parks and playing fields on the riverbank near the bridge. Expect to be part of a large and enthusiastic crowd as you enjoy performances by established world music, rock and folk bands from Wales, Ireland and far beyond, including strong representation from the thriving Welsh-language music scene.
• The town is signed from the A470 and A494.
Phone: 08712 301314
www.sesiwnfawr.co.uk

Left: **Bryn Terfel's Faenol Festival.** Combines musical excellence with the most scenic of surroundings.

Where to eat and stay

Alphabetical listing with contact details of restaurants and accommodation

Bistro Conwy, Conwy
Phone: 01492 596326
www.bistroconwy.com

Bodysgallen Hall*, Llandudno
Phone: 01492 584466
www.bodysgallen.com

Brasserie, Ye Olde Bull's Head*,
Beaumaris
Phone: 01248 810329
www.bullsheadinn.co.uk

Bryn Tyrch*, Betws-y-coed
Phone: 01690 720223
www.bryntyrch-hotel.co.uk

Castle Cottage*, Harlech
Phone: 01766 780479
www.castlecottageharlech.co.uk

Castle Hotel, Shakespeares Restaurant*, Conwy
Phone: 01492 582800
www.castlewales.co.uk

Granvilles, Criccieth
Phone: 01766 522506

Le Gallois, Penmaenmawr
Phone: 01492 623820

Lobster Pot*, Nr Holyhead
Phone: 01407 730241
www.thelobsterpot.info

Maes-y-Neuadd*, Talsarnau
Phone: 01766 780200
www.neuadd.com

Penhelig Arms*, Aberdovey
Phone: 01654 767215
www.penheligarms.com

Plas Bodegroes*, Pwllheli
Phone: 01758 612363
www.bodegroes.co.uk

Porth Tocyn Hotel*, Abersoch
Phone: 01758 713303
www.porth-tocyn-hotel. co.uk

Hotel Portmeirion*, Portmeirion
Phone: 01766 772440
www.portmeirion-village.com

Queen's Head*, Nr Penrhyn Bay
Phone: 01492 546570

Stables Bar Restaurant, Mold
Phone: 01352 840577
www.soughtonhall.co.uk

St Tudno Hotel*, Llandudno
Phone: 01492 874411
www.st-tudno.co.uk

Tan-y-Foel*, Nr Betws-y-coed
Phone: 01690 710507
www.tyfhotel.co.uk

Trearddur Bay Hotel*,
Nr Holyhead
Phone: 01407 860301
www.trearddurbayhotel.co.uk

Tyddyn Llan*, Nr Corwen
Phone: 01490 440264
www.tyddynllan.co.uk

Waterfront, Nr Holyhead
Phone: 01407 860006

Ynyshir Hall*, Nr Machynlleth
Phone: 01654 781209
www.ynyshir-hall.co.uk

* Accommodation available

Information and useful websites

Tourist Information Centres throughout Wales have expert and welcoming staff who can offer independent assistance with planning routes, booking accommodation and the search for information on places or events to visit. They are your one-stop shop for holiday and short-break information, late availability and last-minute offers.

For a full list of Tourist Information Centres www.visitwales.com

Tourist Information Centres:
The Isle of Anglesey
T 01248 713177

Snowdonia Mountains and Coast/Eryri Mynyddoedd a Môr
T 01690 710426

Llandudno, Colwyn Bay, Rhyl and Prestatyn
T 01492 876413

The North Wales Borderlands
T 01978 860828

Useful websites

Castles and heritage:
www.cadw.wales.gov.uk
www.nationaltrust.org.uk
www.bbc.co.uk/wales/history
www.bodnantgarden.co.uk

Museums and galleries:
www.museumwales.ac.uk
www.cymal.wales.gov.uk
(national and local museums)
www.bodelwyddan-castle.co.uk
(including National Portrait Gallery)

Festivals and events:
www.eisteddfod.org.uk
(the National Eisteddfod of Wales)
www.international-eisteddfod.co.uk
(Llangollen Eisteddfod)
www.urdd.org (Urdd Youth Eisteddfod)
www.brynfest.com
(Bryn Terfel's Faenol Festival)
www.artswales.org.uk
(Arts Council of Wales)
www.thingstodo.org.uk
www.homecomingwales.com

Other websites
www.portmeirion-village.com
www.ccw.gov.uk (National Trails)
www.llgc.org.uk
(National Library of Wales)
www.visitwales.com
www.wales.gov.uk
www.nationalparks.gov.uk
www.gwynedd.gov.uk
www.conwy.gov.uk
www.denbighshire.gov.uk
www.flintshire.gov.uk

How to get here

By car. The UK's road network serves visitors to Wales well, making it easy to get to by car. In the north the A55 coastal Expressway provides a trouble-free, fast route to the north coast.

By train. Wales is easy to get to from all of the UK. From London Euston there is a service that will take you to Bangor in four hours. It also takes around two hours to get from Manchester to the resort of Llandudno on Wales's north coast.

If you are visiting from overseas you will find that there are good links between all major airports and the main rail network. For rail enquiries and booking ring + 44(0) 8457 48 49 50 or visit one of the following websites: www.nationalrail.co.uk, www.thetrainline.com or www.qjump.co.uk

By coach or bus. National Express offers a nationwide service of fast, reliable express coaches. There is a good service from London Victoria coach station to many towns and cities in Wales as well as from many cities and towns in both England and Scotland. For example, the journey time between London and Wrexham is around six hours. There are also convenient Flightlink coach services from major airports to destinations in Wales. For information and bookings call
+ 44 (0) 8705 808080 or go to:
www.nationalexpress.co.uk
Inside Wales there is an extensive network of regional and local bus services.

By air. There are regular direct flights to Cardiff International Airport from a wide range of destinations, including Amsterdam, Cork, Glasgow, London City, Paris and Prague. Also, Amsterdam, Dublin and Paris act as gateway hubs for European and international flights. For flight information call
+44 (0) 1446 711111
email infodesk@cwl.aero or visit
www.cial.co.uk
London's airports and those at Birmingham and Manchester are all good gateways to Wales. Each has good road and rail connections.

By sea. Two ferry companies operate services between north Wales and Ireland. They are:
Irish Ferries. Dublin to Holyhead, Tel: +44 (0) 8705 171717
www.irishferries.com
Stena Line. Dun Laoghaire or Dublin to Holyhead.
Tel: +44 (0) 8705 707070
www.stenaline.co.uk

Other ferry ports (along England's south coast and elsewhere) have good cross-country motorway and main road links to Wales. For car travellers arriving on the EuroTunnel service it is motorway all the way from Dover to Wales.

Castles and heritage throughout Wales

Most of the many archaeological sites, castles and historic houses of Wales, and numerous former centres of industry, are in the care of one of two agencies – Cadw or the National Trust. It is said that if a historic property has a roof, then it is likely to be run by the National Trust; otherwise it is probably the responsibility of Cadw. Not an infallible guide, of course, but a helpful start.

Wales has more castles and fortifications for its area than anywhere else in Europe.

Wales has more castles and fortifications for its area than anywhere else in Europe. If you include every earthwork revealed by archaeological surveys and aerial photography, there are more than six hundred sites. Their number and variety reflect the nation's turbulent and fascinating history.

In prehistoric times, life was a constant struggle for survival against the elements and attack by others. The earliest inhabitants of Wales made stone tools and weapons, but their limited building abilities were mainly directed at ceremonial matters and the commemoration of their dead. Though primitive fortifications exist, they are not substantial.

The **Celtic tribes**, who lived throughout what we now call the UK and Ireland before the arrival of the **Romans**, were notoriously warlike. The landscape – especially coastal promontories and hilltops with good views – is peppered with the remains of their substantial forts.

Above: **Chirk Castle.** The last of the castles built by Edward I in his conquest of Wales, Chirk Castle has fantastic gardens and a stunning view over nine counties.

The Romans introduced a sophisticated network of forts, barracks, roads and ports to sustain their legions as they encountered the troublesome tribes of the region they called **Cambria**. Many indigenous **Celts** eventually saw the advantage of adopting Roman ways, and their pragmatic co-operation made possible the governance of this remote extremity of the empire.

When the Romans began pulling out of their distant province of Britannia towards the end of the 4th century, the power vacuum was filled by regional rulers who provided the inspiration for the legendary **King Arthur**, mentioned for the first time in an early Welsh poem and later idealised into a paragon of chivalry.

The Saxons conquered much of what is now England but found Wales and Scotland fiercely resistant. During the 8th century, the eponymous **King Offa of Mercia** ordered the building of his dyke, a low earthwork that marked the western limit of his ambition and recognised the separateness of Wales.

On the Welsh side of **Offa's Dyke**, regional kings and princes consolidated their rule. Their courts were usually peripatetic and their households – families, soldiers, servants, minstrels and poets – moved between several castles. Through war, treaty and marriage their territories began to coalesce into an emerging Welsh nation.

In 1039, **Gruffudd ap Llywelyn** became the first ruler of a united and independent Welsh nation that was organised upon a sophisticated legal and constitutional foundation. But this was not the best timing. Within a couple of decades of the arrival of **William the Conqueror** in 1066, the **Normans** had taken the lands and powers of the Welsh princes in much of south-eastern Wales and were extending their influence and building their solid castles throughout the lowlands.

In 1267, **Llywelyn ap Gruffudd** was recognised by **Henry III as Prince of Wales**, but this harmonious arrangement was also short-lived. The English king **Edward I**, who came to power in 1272, aimed to bring Wales and Scotland fully under his rule. He spent vast sums in building his 'iron ring' of castles around Gwynedd, from where Llywelyn mounted his campaigns to retain

Clockwise from top left:
Gwydir Castle interior and exterior. Regarded as the finest Tudor house in Wales, Gwydir Castle was once the home to Katheryn of Berain, cousin of Elizabeth I.
Caldey Abbey. Caldey has been home to various orders of monks since Celtic times. Today the picturesque monastery overlooks the pretty island cottages, Village Green and Shop.
Tenby Tudor Merchant's House. This late 15th century town house is furnished to recreate the atmosphere of family life in Tudor times.

independence. Having succeeded in securing solid support throughout Wales against overwhelming forces, Llywelyn was eventually ambushed and killed at Cilmeri near Builth Wells in 1282.

Numerous fortified mansions and grand homes in the style of medieval castles have been built in Wales since those distant days of strife, but the pinnacle of castle building for military purposes was in the time of Edward I. The remarkable architecture and ingenuity of four of his castles – **Caernarfon, Conwy, Harlech** and **Beaumaris** – built by Master James of St George, the French genius in such matters, has been recognised in their collective designation as a UNESCO World Heritage Site.

Until the mid-18th century, Wales was a largely rural nation where landowners enjoyed the resources to build fine houses, and agricultural workers and their families lived modestly. The coastline was dotted with small harbours where fishing was the main activity.

The largest structures were the castles, which had long since outlived their purpose, and the great religious buildings, including the ruins of medieval abbeys.

The Industrial Revolution rapidly transformed the working pattern, the economy, the built environment and the social fabric of Wales. Within a few decades,

small towns and villages were transformed into some of the largest concentrations of industry in the world.

Merthyr Tydfil became the world's largest iron-producing centre, making possible the building of the railways. A pall of noxious fumes over **Swansea** and **Llanelli** reflected their specialisation in the smelting of copper, tin and other metals. Large numbers of people flocked to Wales from England and further afield, to provide manpower for the new industries.

The mining of coal in the south Wales Valleys boomed to the point where, by the early 20th century, 250,000 men toiled underground and **Cardiff** became the world's largest coal-exporting port. By this time, the combined population of the mining towns of the south Wales Valleys was equivalent – in number and variety of origin – to that of an additional large city.

Previous page: **Conwy Castle.** The castle's well-preserved walls give visitors the opportunity to walk along the top portions of the castle towers and town walls.

Above left: **Caerphilly Castle.** The castle was a revolutionary masterpiece of 13th century military planning due to its immense size (1.2h) and its large-scale use of water for defence.

Above right: **Menai Bridge.** At the time it was completed, Thomas Telford's bridge was the largest suspension bridge in the world.

The slate quarries of north and mid Wales expanded to meet the demand for roofing material at home, in Europe and in north America. Seaports grew to handle the thriving trade in raw materials and goods – and, as the railway network grew, to serve the passenger traffic to and from Ireland. Manufacturing industry expanded, particularly in south-eastern and north-eastern Wales.

Many of the industrial buildings and structures that made this ferment of activity possible – along with the grand houses built on its wealth – may be visited today. These heritage sites provide a fascinating insight into the way the people of Wales lived and worked in times gone by.

Several sites of the National Museum Wales (please see overleaf) provide especially direct insights into the industries that were so significant in shaping the appearance of the land and the character of the people.

Above: **Basingwerk Abbey.** During the 13th century Anglo-Welsh wars, Basingwerk's sympathies lay with the English. It apparently suffered little, and by the later 15th century had become quite prosperous. It was dissolved in 1536.

Left: **Bodnant Garden.** Spanning some 80 acres, Bodnant Garden is one of the most beautiful gardens in the UK.

Museums and galleries throughout Wales

In addition to the National Museums, you will find that most towns have a museum or heritage centre dedicated to the extraordinary variety of life and culture to be found in this deeply fascinating part of the world.

As befits a nation with such a rich history and well-preserved material heritage, Wales has many excellent museums.

As befits a nation with such a rich history and well-preserved material heritage, Wales has many excellent museums.

The **National Museum Wales** is a widely dispersed group of leading institutions. The **National Slate Museum** in Llanberis, tells how the quarrymen extracted the versatile building and roofing material from the mountains, and describes their tough lives. The

National Wool Museum in the Teifi valley is the place to try carding and spinning for yourself, and to learn all about wool production and use.

Few museums offer anything quite as dramatic as the underground tour at the **Big Pit National Coal Museum** near Blaenavon. And few put information technology to such

Above left: **Oriel Mostyn Gallery.**
The Oriel Mostyn Gallery in Llandudno north Wales is one the UK's premier contemporary, modern and fine art galleries.
Above right: **National Museum Cardiff.** The National Museum Cardiff houses one of Europe's finest art collections as well as preserving some of the nation's treasures.

effective use as the **National Waterfront Museum** in Swansea, which tells the story of the people of Wales at work, in industries old and new.

St Fagans National History Museum is one of Europe's very best open-air museums, featuring a wonderful collection of buildings relocated from all over Wales, together with absorbing indoor exhibitions about rural life and folk traditions.

The **National Museum Cardiff** is the nation's storehouse of all that is best in many and varied fields of interest – from archaeology to zoology, decorative arts, fine art, geology, science, technology and many other areas.

In addition to the National Museums, you will find that most towns have a museum or heritage centre dedicated to the extraordinary variety of life and culture to be found in this deeply fascinating part of the world.

Interesting museums include the **Llangollen Motor Museum** and **Pendine Museum of Speed**, the **National Coracle Centre**, which displays coracles from all over the world, the **Rhondda Heritage Park** and the **Blaenavon World Heritage Museum**, a testimony to the pre-eminence of south Wales as the world's major producer of iron and coal in the 19th century.

Wales has a long tradition of artistic expression, which continues today. Many gifted

artists and craftspersons live and work here and their work is sold from galleries and studios across the land. Collections of fine art, from Wales and elsewhere, have been assembled both by the nation and by individual collectors.

Collections of fine art, from Wales and elsewhere, have been assembled both by the nation and by individual collectors.

National Museum Cardiff displays many treasures including a significant collection of Impressionist works by Renoir, Monet and Cézanne. Eminent Welsh artists also feature, including 18th century landscape pioneers Richard Wilson and Thomas Jones, and 20th century artists Augustus John, Gwen John and Ceri Richards.

The **National Portrait Gallery** in Wales has over 100 portraits from the 19th century collections including works by John Singer Sargent and the Pre-Raphaelites.

The **Turner House Gallery** in Penarth shows fine art of the highest quality.

Above: **National Portrait Gallery.** The National Portrait Gallery at Bodelwyddan Castle houses many wonderful portraits from the 19th century.

The westernmost regions of Wales (especially Anglesey, Snowdonia and Pembrokeshire) have inspired many artists. Look out for pleasing depictions of landscape, seascape, the seasons and rural life by Sir Kyffin Williams RA, William Selwyn, Rob Piercy, John Knapp-Fisher, Donald McIntyre and others.

Clusters of high-quality artists' studios may be found at Glynllifon (near Caernarfon), Ruthin, Hay-on-Wye and St Clears.

The biennial **Artes Mundi** competition at the **National Museum Cardiff** features the work of international conceptual artists.

Above left: **St Fagans.**
St Fagans Castle with its splendid Rose Garden is only one of many buildings you can explore in this informative open-air museum. Step back in time as far as the Iron Age and experience how Welsh people once lived and worked.

Above right: **National Waterfront Museum.** At the National Museum Wales's newest attraction you can experience noise, grime, high finance, upheaval, consumerism and opportunity and see how Wales's Industrial Revolution help shape the rest of the world.

Left: **Aberystwyth Arts Centre.**
The award-winning Aberystwyth Arts Centre has a wide-ranging programme of events and activities across all art forms. It is recognised as a national centre for arts development and welcomes over 650,000 visitors a year through their doors.

Festivals and events throughout Wales

There are festivals in Wales for just about every aspect of culture. You will find everything from large national events to local musical and literary festivals, carnivals, regattas and shows that draw the crowds to historic villages, towns and harbours.

You will find everything from large national events to local musical and literary festivals, carnivals, regattas and shows that draw the crowds to historic villages, towns and harbours.

The main tourism season in Wales extends from Easter onwards, through the summer, until the school term begins in early September. Countless events, suitable for all the family, are organised during these months. Many places also provide ample reason to visit throughout the year, by organising activities and entertainment appropriate to autumn, Christmas, and other times.

Above left: **Aberystwyth and Ceredigion County Show.** This County Show is one of many across Wales that promote agriculture and bring together the farming industry and the local community. Shows like these hold a number of events that make great days out for visitors.
Above right: **The Big Cheese, Caerphilly.** This is an annual celebration of local and Welsh heritage, history, culture and entertainment. The festival includes jugglers, fire eaters, living history re-enactments, music, funfair rides and more.

Musical, literary and theatrical enthusiasms feature strongly and you will find performances at every level from professional venue to village hall. The orchestra of **Welsh National Opera** and the **BBC National Orchestra of Wales** appear at spectacular open-air concerts each summer; at Swansea's Proms in the Park, Cardiff Bay and elsewhere.

Musical styles ranging from classical to brass bands, and from jazz to folk and roots music, have strong followings at festivals, halls and clubs across the land. Authentic Welsh folk traditions, including music and dance, are still celebrated, notably in and around Cardiff, at the beginning of May and at Christmas and New Year.

The traditions of the countryside are a recurrent theme, central to the identity of many Welsh people. Despite the demands of the farming life, the seasonal pattern allows time for the agricultural shows at local and national level. The largest of these, the **Royal Welsh Agricultural Show** is held at Builth Wells during **July**, with the **Winter Fair** following at the same venue early in **December**. Smaller shows, to which all are welcome, are organised at county level throughout Wales.

Some of the more vigorous, and occasionally dangerous, traditional sports have disappeared but Wales has made a unique contribution in this area

of endeavour. The little town of **Llanwrtyd Wells** has become famous for its calendar of what can only be described as profoundly wacky challenges, including the **world bog-snorkelling championships**! The latter requires an unusual ability to ignore the cold and unsavoury surroundings, and to navigate in zero visibility, as you swim as rapidly as you can for the finish line.

The largest annual events arrive one after the other during the spring, summer and early autumn. Typically organised by experienced professionals supported by resourceful local committees, they feature big names in their respective fields and provide a visitor experience second-to-none.

Llanwrtyd Wells has become famous for its world bog- snorkelling championships!

Above: **Welsh National Opera at Cardiff Bay.** The Oval Basin at Cardiff Bay hosts fabulous open-air concerts by big names, including Welsh National Opera, as well as being a venue for other events such as Cardiff's International Food and Drink Festival.

The Hay Festival of Literature, held each May, sees world-famous authors, and enthusiastic readers.

The **Hay Festival of Literature**, held each **May**, sees world-famous authors, and enthusiastic readers who appreciate a good book, congregating at the small town of Hay-on-Wye, which has more than 30 bookshops.

Brecon pulsates to the sounds of jazz during **August**, when traditional bands and skilled solo practitioners of the more rarified forms come to town for the **Brecon Jazz Festival**.

Bryn Terfel, the world's leading bass-baritone, invites world-class guests to join him on stage before an enthusiastic home audience at his annual **Faenol Festival** (voted Best Show in Wales) held near Bangor each **August** Bank Holiday.

The Cardiff Festival offers an exciting series of concerts throughout the summer.

The **Cardiff Festival** offers an exciting series of concerts, a multicultural carnival, a harbour festival, food shows, sports competitions and many other events throughout the summer, in the city centre and at Cardiff Bay.

Celebrations of food and produce, including the **Abergavenny Food Festival**, make a point of inviting local companies to provide the best possible food and drink – both home-produced and more exotic.

The largest of Wales's cultural festivals – in fact, one of the largest in Europe, with a daily attendance typically exceeding 20,000 – is the **National Eisteddfod**. This week-long gathering follows a tradition established by Lord Rhys at Cardigan Castle in 1176, whereby poets and musicians (and nowadays many other talented and creative participants) meet in a spirit of friendly competition.

Clockwise from top left:
Hay Literature Festival. This world-renowned literary festival hosts talks and book signings of the biggest names of the time. Authors from around the world come here to promote their new books. A must for book-lovers.
Brecon Jazz Festival. One of the best jazz festivals in Europe and all the tickets to see the big names performing will go fast. Even if you don't have a ticket, you can soak up the Festival's vibrant atmosphere.
Abergavenny Food Festival. Eagerly awaited by foodies, the Abergavenny Food Festival is one of the largest in the UK.

The largest of Wales's cultural festivals – in fact, one of the largest in Europe, with a daily attendance typically exceeding 20,000 – is the National Eisteddfod.

Held at the beginning of **August**, the **National Eisteddfod** moves to a different part of Wales each year. The enormous pavilion, venue for competitions and evening concerts, seats some 3,500 people. The surrounding Maes, or campus, has several smaller performance and exhibition spaces and upwards of 300 stands, where most of Wales's cultural and educational organisations are represented.

The central point of the **National Eisteddfod** is that everything happens in the Welsh language. Simultaneous-translation receivers are available at the main entrance and anyone wishing to learn the language will be made welcome at the Learners' Pavilion – there's a hotly contested prize for Welsh Learner of the Year.

The principle of friendly competition has been extended worldwide by the **Llangollen International Musical Eisteddfod**. This captivating multicultural gathering originated in 1947 as a means of bringing together like-

minded people from all over war-ravaged Europe. One of its most moving moments being the first appearance by a choir from Germany in 1949. Performers of appropriately high ability nowadays travel from all over the world to attend in a spirit of shared appreciation.

Little wonder then, that this is the only festival in the world to have been nominated for the Nobel Peace Prize.

Performers of appropriately high ability nowadays travel from all over the world to attend in a spirit of shared appreciation.

Above left: **Royal Welsh Show.** The Royal Welsh Show is one of the most prestigious events of its type in Europe, and brings to together the farming industry and rural community in a celebration of the best of British agriculture with a unique and very special 'Welsh' flavour.

Above right: **Cardiff Festival.** Cardiff Festival is the UK's largest free outdoor festival, and brings colour and cultural vibrancy to the city and the waterfront area of Cardiff Bay.

The Welsh language
The ancient language of Wales is very much alive during the 21st century and is spoken by around half a million people.

Welsh evolved from the Celtic languages spoken throughout Britain at the time of the Roman occupation. These included two distinct forms: the Goidelic group, which produced the Irish, Scots Gaelic and Manx (Isle of Man) languages, and the Brythonic group, from which the Welsh, Cornish and Breton languages emerged.

Welsh is one of Europe's oldest languages and is by far the strongest survivor of all the Celtic tongues. As with all languages, it has over many centuries absorbed words and influences from elsewhere.

There is no compulsion to speak Welsh but many people deeply enjoy doing so. The lyrical nature of the language seems designed to produce pleasingly poetic sounds and opens the door to a treasure trove of culture. Even the smallest attempt at learning the basics will be much appreciated by the people you meet, even if they need to help you a little with some of the pronunciation.

The language is generally phonetic, so that each letter represents only one sound: what is written is what you say. Some of the sounds however differ from English, as follows:

'a' as in 'apple'
'e' as in 'exit'
'i' as in 'ee'
'o' as in office
'u' sounds similar to the 'i' in 'win', but longer
'w' as in 'win' - serves as a vowel
'y' as the 'u' in 'cup', but longer – serves as a vowel
the famous 'll' is akin to the 'tl' sound in the English words 'antler' or 'Bentley'- but you breathe out gently as you say it.
the Welsh 'ch' is similar to that in Johann Sebastian Bach, a highly regarded figure in Wales!
'dd' sounds like the 'th' in then
'th' sounds like the 'th' in thing

Websites
www.bwrdd-yr-iaith.org.uk (information on the Welsh language)
www.bbc.co.uk/wales/learnwelsh

A few helpful words and phrases

Good morning	Bore da
Good afternoon	Prynhawn da
Goodbye	Hwyl fawr
Good evening	Noswaith dda
Good health!/Cheers	Iechyd da!
Good night	Nos da
How are you?	Sut mae?
Very good	Da iawn
Welcome	Croeso
Welcome to Wales	Croeso i Gymru
fine thanks	iawn diolch
yes	ie
no	na
please	os gwelwch yn dda
Thank you	Diolch
Good	Da
small	bach
big	mawr
where is?	ble mae?
castle	castell
river	afon
food	bwyd
drink	diod
I'd like a pint of...	Hoffwn i beint o...
And a glass of...	a gwydriad o...
Where am I?	Ble ydw i?
I'm lost!	Dwi ar goll!
Where's the nearest cashpoint?	Ble mae'r twll yn y wal agosaf?

Graffeg books

Graffeg publish illustrated books about contemporary life in Wales. Each book is focused on a particular interest: landscapes, food, lifestyle, heritage, architecture, festivals, music, arts, sports and culture. Graffeg books make wonderful guides, travelling companions and gifts.

View our catalogue online www.graffeg.com

Visit our website for the latest news and view the Graffeg book list online @ ww.graffeg.com Browse through books online before you order.

Published by Graffeg.
Tel: 029 2037 7312
sales@graffeg.com
www.graffeg.com

About the authors

Written by
David Williams

David Williams is a writer and photographer having a wide-ranging knowledge of the life, culture and history of Wales. He wrote, and supplied images for, the Graffeg books Landscape Wales, About Cardiff and About Wales – and for other titles in this series of pocket guides. He works for numerous book and magazine publishers, broadcasters, tourism authorities and cultural organisations. A graduate of the University of Wales, he is a fluent Welsh speaker.

As a contributor to Photolibrary Wales, his images help to promote Wales worldwide. Having travelled throughout Wales, he is thoroughly familiar with its people and places, and able to offer a balanced perspective on the whole of our compact but enormously fascinating nation.

Foreword by
Siân Lloyd

Originally from Neath, Siân Lloyd attended school in Ystalyfera and studied at the universities of Cardiff and Oxford. She worked as a television presenter with S4C, and as a radio and television journalist, before joining the ITV national weather team. She reports on the environment for ITN, and on travel and environmental matters for national newspapers.

Her wide spectrum of television appearances, as presenter and guest, includes children's programmes, quizzes, chat shows, talent shows, consumer programmes and current-affairs discussions. Her interests include food – cooking it, eating it, and writing and making programmes about it! – mountain walking (from Wales to the Alps), chess, Scrabble, films and theatre.

Index

A

Aberconwy House 33
Abersoch Jazz Festival 84
Alice in Wonderland Centre 37
Amlwch 13
Amlwch Port 13
Amlwch Viking Festival 27
Anglesey County Show 27
Anglesey Oyster and Welsh Food Fair 27

B

Bala Lake Railway 83
Bangor 69
Barclodiad y Gawres, Rhosneigr 19
Bardsey Island 69
Basingwerk Abbey 49
Beaumaris 14
Beaumaris Castle 13, 14
Beaumaris Festival 29
Beaumaris Gaol and Courthouse 17
Beddgelert 70
Bersham Heritage Centre Inn Works 62
Betws-y-Coed 71
Blaenau Ffestiniog 72
Bodelwyddan 45
Bodelwyddan Castle 45
Bodnant Garden 41
Brass Rubbing Centre 32
Britannia Bridge 17
Bryn Celli Ddu 19
Bryn Terfel's Faenol Festival 84

C

Caernarfon 73
Caernarfon – Victoria Dock 73
Caernarfon Castle 74
Castell Dinas Brân 52, 54
Castell y Bere 83
Cemaes Celtic Festival 29
Chirk 46
Chirk Castle 46
Clwyd Theatr Cymru 56
Clywedog Valley 62
Colwyn Bay 31
Conwy – suspension bridge 35
Conwy Castle 31

Conwy 31
Conwy Visitor Centre 32
Corris 76
Corwen 46
Criccieth 76
Criccieth Castle 76
Criccieth Festival 85
Cwm Croesor 71

D

Denbigh 47
Denbigh Castle 47
Denbigh Midsummer Festival 67
Din Lligwy 24
Dolbadarn Castle 77
Dolwyddelan Castle 71

E

Ellin's Tower 27
Erddig Hall 62

F

Ffestiniog Railway 83
Flint 49
Flint Castle 49
Flintshire Festival 64

G

Gŵyl Bwyd Môr Llŷn Seafood Festival 85
Gŵyl Cadi Ha 65
Galeri 73
Gallery 103 at NEWI 62
Gop cairn at Trelawnyd 60
Great Orme Bronze Age copper mines 35
Great Orme Marine Drive 35
Great Orme tramway 35
Greenfield Valley 49
Greenfield Valley Heritage Park 50
Gwydir Castle 79

H

H M Stanley exhibition 49
Harbour at Rhos-on-Sea 41
Harlech 77
Harlech Castle 77
Hawarden 50
Holyhead 21
Holyhead Maritime Festival 29

Holyhead Maritime Museum 22
Holyhead Roman fort 21
Holywell 51
Home Front Experience, The 37, 38

I

Inigo Jones Slate Works 74
Island Arts Week, Anglesey 29

K

King Arthur's Labyrinth, Corris 76

L

Llanberis 77
Llandudno Festival of Music and the Arts 42
Llandudno 35
Llandudno Museum 37
Llandudno pier and promenade 35
Llandudno Victorian Extravaganza and Transport Festival 43
Llandudno Victorian Town Trail 37
Llanfairpwllgwyngyllgogerychwyrndrobwllllantysiliogogogoch 20
Llangar Church 46
Llangernyw 41
Llangollen 52
Llangollen canal 52
Llangollen International Musical Eisteddfod 62, 65
Llangollen Motor Museum 53
Llangollen Steam Railway 53
Llanrwst 79
Llanrwst Almshouses 79
Llechwedd Slate Caverns 72
Llynnon Mill 23
Llys Rhosyr, Newborough 20

M

Menai Suspension Bridge 17
Minera Leadmines 62
Moelfre 14
Mold 56
Mostyn Gallery 38
Museum of Childhood Memories, Beaumaris 17

N

Nant Gwrtheyrn 81
National Portrait Gallery,
Bodelwyddan 45
National Slate Museum 78
North Wales Country Music Festival 38
North Wales International Jazz Guitar Festival 66
North Wales International Music Festival 66

O

Open-air theatre at Plas Newydd 18
Oriel Mostyn Gallery 38
Oriel Ynys Môn 19

P

Padarn Lake Railway 83
Pantasaph Friary 52
Parys Mountain 13
Pavilion Theatre, Rhyl 41
Penmon 25
Penmon Priory 25
Penrhyn Castle 69
Pilgrim's Route to Bardsey 70
Plas Mawr, Conwy 33
Plas Newydd, Anglesey 18
Plas Newydd, Llangollen 55
Plas yn Rhiw 81
Portmeirion 81
Professor Codman's Punch and Judy Show 39

R

Red Dragon Heritage Centre 70
Regional Print Centre 61
Rhiw 81
Rhos-on-Sea 41
Rhosllanerchrugog Miners' Institute 64
Rhuddlan 56
Rhuddlan Castle 56
Rhyl 41
Roman fort Segontium 74
Roman fort, Holyhead 21
Royal Cambrian Academy 32
Rug Chapel 46
Ruthin 58
Ruthin Castle 58
Ruthin Craft Centre 59
Ruthin Festival 67
Ruthin Gaol 58

Index

S

Saint Trillo's Chapel, Rhos-on-Sea 41
Sesiwn Fawr Dolgellau 85
Sir Henry Jones Museum 41
Smallest House in Britain 32
Snowdonia railways 83
South Stack 25
St Asaph 59
St Asaph Cathedral 59
St Deiniol's Library, Hawarden 50
St Giles's Church, Wrexham 62
St Margaret's Church,
Bodelwyddan 45
St Mary's Abbey, Bardsey 69
St Winefride's Well 51
Swtan, restored cottage 24
Sygun Copper Mine 70

T

Tal-y-cafn 41
Talyllyn Railway 83
Theatr Colwyn 31
Theatr Twm o'r Nant, Denbigh 49
Tre'r Ceiri 83
Trefriw 42
Trefriw Woollen Mill and Spa 42
Trelawnydd 60
Tŷ Mawr 24
Tŷ Mawr Wybrnant 72
Tywyn 83

U

Ucheldre Centre, Holyhead 22

V

Valle Crucis Abbey 56
Venue Cymru 37

W

Welsh Highland Railway, Snowdon 83
Wrexham 61
Wrexham Arts Centre 61
Wrexham Arts Festival 67

Y

Y Capel Art Gallery 54
Yale Memorial Gallery 61